CW01209467

Other counties in this series include:

BUCKINGHAMSHIRE	HAMPSHIRE
CHESHIRE	LEICESTERSHIRE
DERBYSHIRE	LINCOLNSHIRE
DEVON	SUFFOLK
DORSET	SURREY
ESSEX	SUSSEX

First published 1998
© Photographs, Bill Meadows 1998
© Text, David Green 1998

All rights reserved
No reproduction permitted
without the prior permission
of the publisher:

COUNTRYSIDE BOOKS
3 CATHERINE ROAD
NEWBURY, BERKSHIRE

ISBN 1 85306 537 4

Photograph on page 1 shows Aston Cantlow, near Alcester
Photograph on page 5 shows Holy Trinity church, Stratford-upon-Avon

Designed by Mon Mohan
Produced through MRM Associates Ltd, Reading
Printed in Singapore

WARWICKSHIRE

A PORTRAIT IN COLOUR

**BILL MEADOWS &
DAVID GREEN**

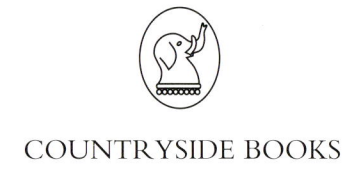

COUNTRYSIDE BOOKS

Contents

Introduction	4	Southam	42
Long Compton and Little Compton	6	Napton-on-the-Hill and Priors Hardwick	44
Feldon Country	8	Draycote Water and Thurlaston	46
Ilmington and Shipston-on-Stour	10	Dunchurch	48
The Fosse Way	12	Rugby	50
Kineton and Edgehill	14	Wolston and King's Newnham	52
Radway and Warmington	16	Coombe Abbey and Brinklow	54
The Burton Dassett Hills	18	Coventry	56
Tysoe and Upton House	20	Berkswell	58
Welford-on-Avon and Bidford-on-Avon	22	Meriden	60
Shakespeare in Trust	24	Packwood House	62
Stratford-upon-Avon	26	Earlswood Lakes	64
Alcester	28	Knowle	66
Henley-in-Arden	30	Solihull	68
Barford	32	Coleshill	70
Warwick	34	Nuneaton	72
Kenilworth	36	Sutton Park	74
Leamington Spa	38	Polesworth and Atherstone	76
Harbury and Long Itchington	40	Newton Regis	78

INTRODUCTION

If one had to encapsulate the character of Warwickshire in a single sentence, the words of the American writer Henry James could hardly be bettered: 'The core and centre of the English world; midmost England, unmitigated England'. It is a county, though, of which outsiders often have a quite mistaken perception. Many years ago when I lived and worked in London, my view of Warwickshire was decidedly blinkered and not a little jaundiced. The fact that it was north of Watford seemed to be a distinct disadvantage, and its proximity on the map to the great Midlands industrial conurbation appeared to do little for its aesthetic quality.

My misconceptions were soon to be emphatically dispelled when I accepted the opportunity, admittedly with some initial trepidation, to make Warwickshire my home. This was almost forty years ago, and in those intervening years I have come to know the county intimately, and to appreciate the extraordinary depth of its roots in English history, the rare character of its towns and villages, and the varied beauty of its countryside.

The controversial boundary changes of 1974 caused Warwickshire to pay a heavy price in terms of land area. It lost its two great cities – Birmingham and Coventry – to the newly created County of West Midlands, together with the historic towns of Solihull and Sutton Coldfield. It also handed over a substantial swathe of countryside dotted with some notable villages. Many Warwickshire people deplored these alterations to the map, and they still do: it's not uncommon, even today, to find residents of the West Midlands doggedly maintaining that their addresses are still in Warwickshire.

Perhaps one day the boundaries will be put back to where they historically belong, but in the meantime they have caused a minor dilemma over the choice of subjects for this book. Should Warwickshire be treated as the present-day county, or the one which existed before 1974? The latter choice has to be the right one, as the places which now find themselves in the West Midlands have, over many centuries, contributed to Warwickshire's history and to the moulding of its character, and they should not therefore be excluded. So in the following pages, the West Midlands county boundary is ignored, although the City of Birmingham itself has not been included, simply because its size and complexity qualify it as a subject on its own.

Any photographic study of a subject as rich in variety as Warwickshire has, inevitably, to be selective in its aim to represent a cross-section of the distinctive facets of town and country, past and present. In this book the county is viewed from south to north, starting with the borderlands adjoining Gloucestershire and Oxfordshire, where the unmistakable character of the Cotswolds spills over into Warwickshire.

This is part of the old Feldon country, a name given to the predominantly agricultural southern half of Warwickshire to distinguish it from the wooded Arden country further north. Nowadays, the distinction between the two areas is less definable, although their traditional characteristics have certainly not disappeared entirely. At least the term Arden lives on as a suffix to the names of various towns and villages, even if most of the trees of the once extensive Forest of Arden have long since disappeared.

Towards the centre of the county lie most of Warwickshire's relatively few towns of any appreciable size: places such as Rugby, far-famed for its school; the elegant spa town of Leamington; historic Warwick, home of the finest medieval castle in England; Kenilworth, whose own castle survives as a majestic ruin; and of course Shakespeare's Stratford-upon-Avon. Linking them all is a landscape of gently rolling farmland, dotted with smaller towns and villages, which reflects the still predominantly rural nature of so much of the county.

Then there's Coventry, which rose phoenix-like after its wartime devastation to give us one of our finest modern cathedrals; and nearby Meriden, reputed to mark the exact centre of England. Bustling Solihull borders the Birmingham conurbation, as does Sutton Coldfield with its 2,500 acres of parkland, and Nuneaton marks the heart of George Eliot country.

Further north again, the ancient hatting town of Atherstone is neighbour to historic Polesworth, until recently an important mining community on the declining Warwickshire coalfield. Onwards from here, and we approach Warwickshire's extreme northern tip where it almost touches Derbyshire. Once again, farming characterises the countryside, and the county's rural quality reasserts itself. There are no more towns, and the villages are few and far between – Warton and Shuttington, Seckington and Austrey, and the most northern one of all, Newton Regis.

Despite all the inevitable sociological and economic pressures which have had to be faced, particularly in the 20th century, quintessential Warwickshire lives on, a little bruised here and there, but with its fair countenance and its richly varied character still largely intact. A flavour of that character is offered in the following pages. I hope it encourages those who are already fortunate enough to live in Warwickshire to appreciate their county a little better, and those who are less familiar with it to fall under its spell – as I have done.

David Green
Leamington Spa

Long Compton and Little Compton

Long Compton is almost the southernmost village in Warwickshire – but not quite. That distinction belongs to neighbouring Little Compton, in a narrow finger of land jutting into Oxfordshire not far from the prehistoric Rollright Stones which sit on a hilltop astride the county boundary.

Local legend has it that these ancient monoliths owe their existence to a malevolent witch who intercepted a travelling king and his followers as they journeyed towards Long Compton, and turned them into stone, before transforming herself into an elder tree. Her successors still allegedly inhabit the area today, and another local legend maintains that 'there are enough witches in Long Compton to draw a wagonload of hay up Long Compton Hill'. If they were to attempt such a foolhardy exercise today, they would have to contend with the traffic thronging the busy tourist route between Oxford and Stratford-upon-Avon which Long Compton straddles.

The long main street, from which the village gets the prefix to its name, is bordered by a pleasing assortment of stone-built cottages, some nestling beneath thatch. Standing invitingly among them is the handsome manor house which now serves as a hotel, and the 18th-century Red Lion Inn. Nearby, the lofty tower of the 13th-century parish church of St Peter and St Paul looks down on one of the most unusual lychgates of any church in Britain (*opposite*). It started life in about 1600 as a two-storey cottage, subsequently having part of its lower storey removed to allow access to the churchyard.

Long Compton has always attracted artists and craftsmen, and among their number in the 1920s was the Reverend William Manton who set up the King's Stone Printing Press, named after that petrified monarch on the nearby hilltop. He acquired something of a national reputation during the general strike of 1926 when, in the absence of newspapers, he used his press to print the *Long Compton Wireless News,* which he distributed by handing copies to passing drivers.

From Long Compton, about three miles of winding country lanes lead to Little Compton, once picturesquely known as Compton-in-the-Flowers. One of its more notable buildings is the Elizabethan manor house, now used as a college, which can claim numerous influential owners in its long history. These included, in the 17th century, Archbishop William Juxon who attended Charles I at his trial and execution, an event commemorated in a window of Little Compton's parish church of St Denys (*inset*).

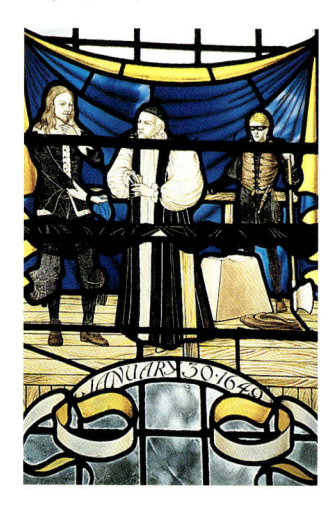

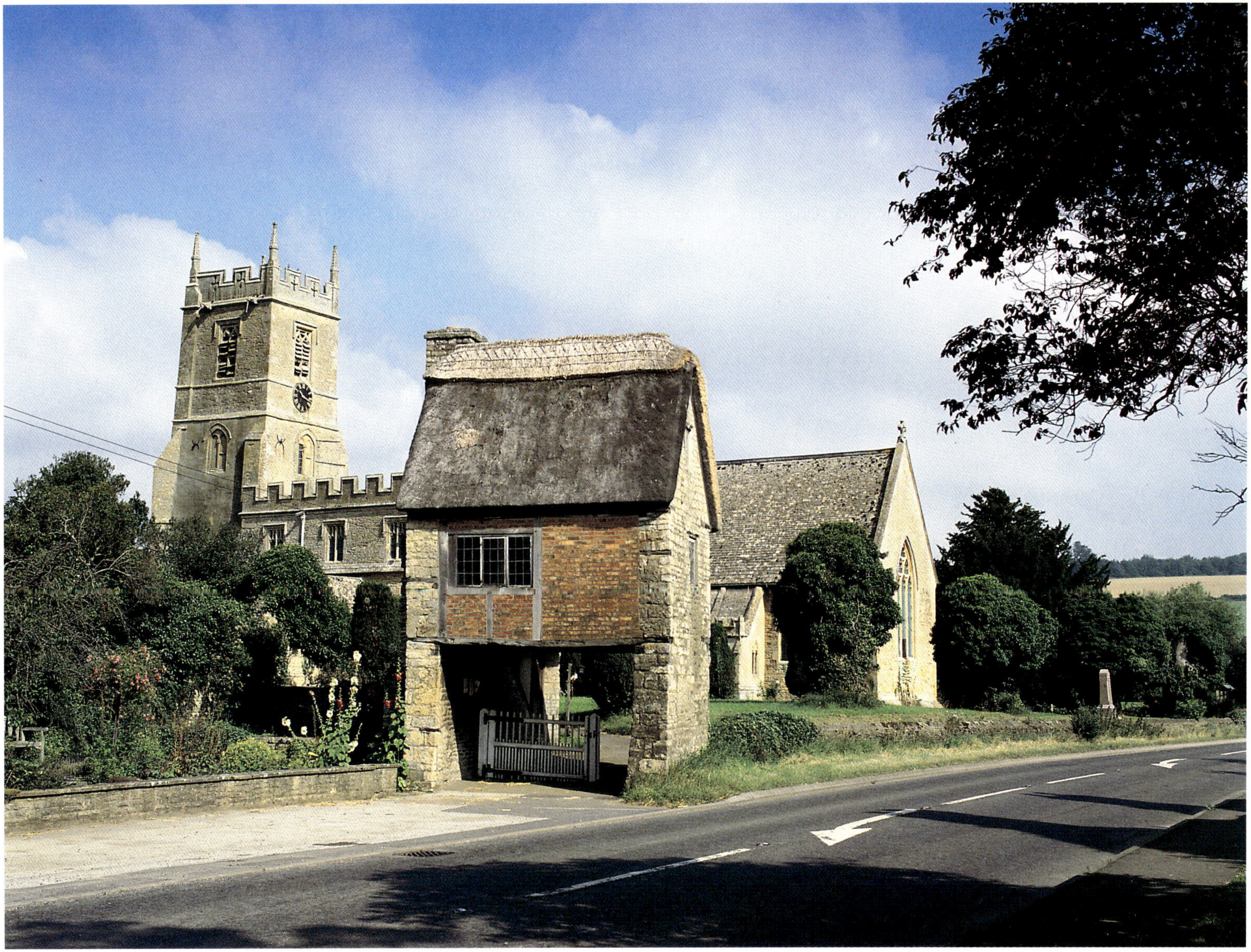

Feldon Country

Historically, the southern part of Warwickshire was known as the Feldon, to distinguish it from Arden, which was the name once given to the land to the north of the river Avon. The terms are rarely used today, but the landscape characteristics from which they were derived can still be appreciated.

The Feldon (from the early English *feld,* or field) was essentially open agricultural land, and Arden was predominantly an area of woodland, immortalised by Shakespeare's Forest of Arden in *As You Like It*. Today, although relatively few trees remain, the name survives in places which retain the 'in-Arden' suffix, like Henley, Hampton and Tanworth. The Feldon has changed less over the centuries, and southernmost Warwickshire is still characterised by rolling farmland, dotted with numerous attractive villages whose roots are set firmly in the fertile land from which their character has been formed over the centuries. The quintessential Feldon panorama pictured (*opposite*) is below Lark Stoke near Ilmington.

Typical among the Feldon's ancient rural communities are places like Barton-on-the-Heath, clustered around its Norman church; Great and Little Wolford, separated by the Nethercote brook; and Cherington and Stourton, Burmington and Willington. The little hamlet of Tidmington must not be ignored either, if only because its diminutive 13th-century church is reputed to be one of the smallest in the Midlands. Eye-catching Ascott and Whichford are here too, the latter now basking in national fame among gardeners as the home of the distinctive terracotta pots produced by Whichford Pottery (*inset*).

Barcheston (or what's left of it after its depopulation following the medieval enclosure acts) is another well-known Feldon name. It was here that the wealthy landowner William Sheldon set up his famous tapestry business in the 16th century.

A few miles away among gentle hills lies remote Winderton, whose neighbours are the three Brailes villages – Sutton-under-Brailes, Upper Brailes and Lower Brailes. The last-named is distinguished by its historic parish church of St George, the aptly named 'cathedral of the Feldon', which contributes yet another strand to the unique character of this wholly delightful region of Warwickshire.

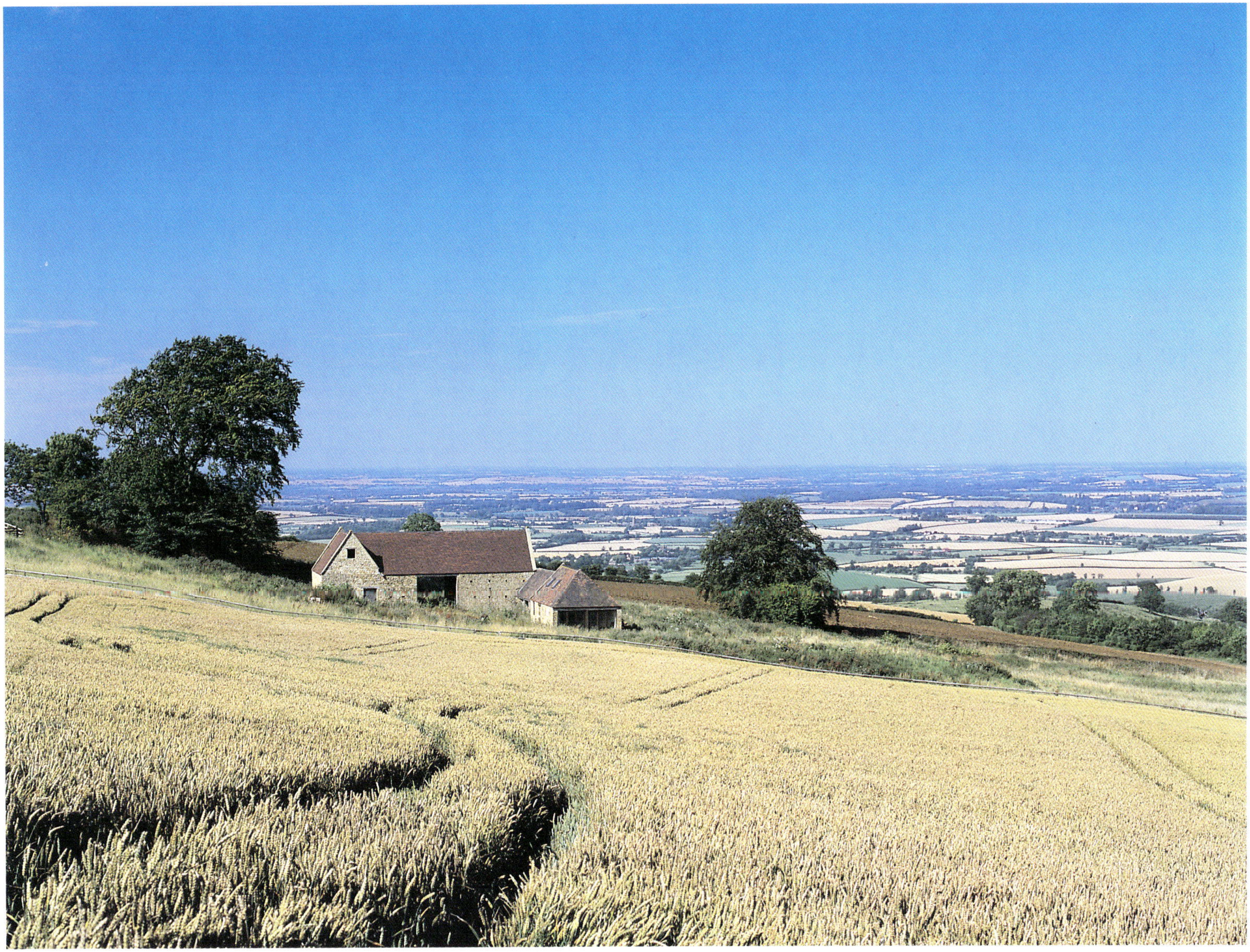

Ilmington and Shipston-on-Stour

Ilmington, one of the larger villages of southern Warwickshire, is a fascinating place, full of history, with an abundance of attractive buildings, many of local stone. It's not surprising that the village has a certain Cotswold air about it, as the surrounding hilly countryside largely consists of outliers of the Cotswolds, one of which is Ilmington Downs, the highest point in Warwickshire at 854 feet. To look down on the village from one of these high vantage points, with the unspoilt Warwickshire countryside stretching away into the distance (*opposite*), is to behold the very essence of rural England at its most sublime.

Ilmington itself has a delightfully casual layout, with lanes and alleyways linked together around a large village green, and the war memorial acting as a symbolic focal point. An old stone fountain commemorates the village's first piped water supply, introduced by the industrious Victorians.

The Norman parish church of St Mary is a notable Ilmington landmark, vying for attention with gabled Ilmington Manor, a fine example of the Cotswold tradition set in beautifully landscaped gardens. Not far away are the village's two popular inns, the Howard Arms, named after the renowned local Howard family, and the Red Lion, formerly the meeting place of the old Court Baron, an influential judicial body which was once an integral part of village life.

Village life today is enriched by the activities of the far-famed Ilmington Morris Men, whose colourful performances enact one of the most evocative traditions of rural England, and delight audiences over a wide area.

A few miles to the south-east of Ilmington lies the small market town of Shipston-on-Stour (*inset*), whose appeal lies in the fact that it has managed to shrug off many of the brasher manifestations of modern urban development. Its name, derived from '*Sheep's* town', is a reminder of the days when one of the busiest sheep markets in the kingdom was held here, while the fine old coaching inns recall Shipston's national importance in the heyday of stagecoach travel. The town's considerable visual appeal is undeniably bolstered by its many elegant Georgian buildings and the fine parish church of St Edmund with its sturdy 15th-century tower standing guard over the main street.

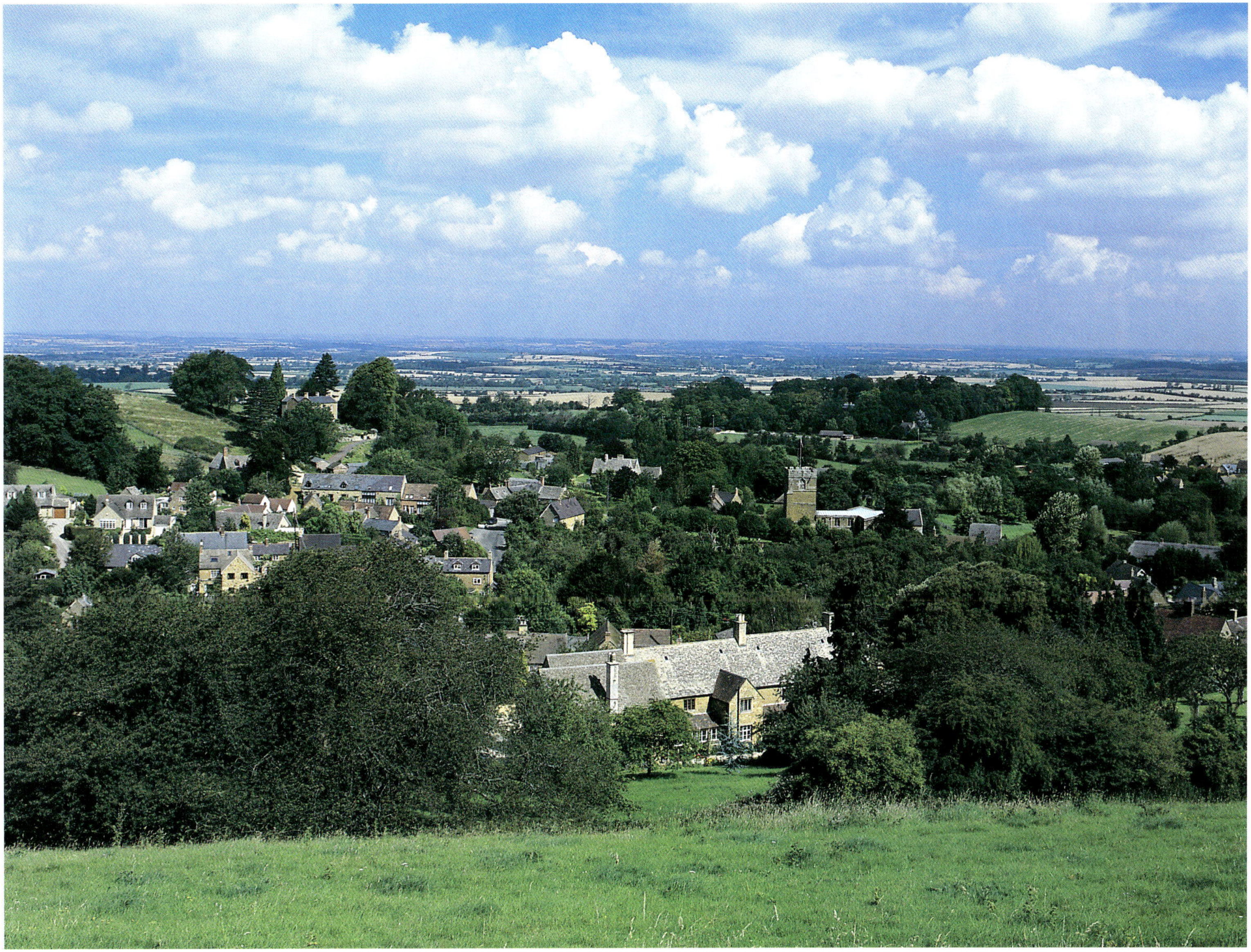

The Fosse Way

The Fosse Way, the remarkable highway built by the Romans from Exeter to Lincoln, enters Warwickshire just to the north of Moreton-in-Marsh and continues on its north-easterly course in a virtually straight line until it meets Watling Street, another great Roman road, at High Cross on the Leicestershire border. Although, to a large extent, superseded by modern trunk roads, it is still an important artery for those living in Warwickshire's rural heartland.

Among the many villages served by the Fosse Way as it traverses the county are three bearing the apt name Stretton (derived from *Street*-town) – Stretton-on-Fosse near the Gloucestershire border; Stretton-on-Dunsmore, where the road crosses the once bleak Dunsmore Heath near Coventry; and Stretton-under-Fosse, a few miles further north, near the point where the Fosse Way now bridges its far more obtrusive modern counterpart, the M6 motorway.

The undulating section pictured (*opposite*) is near the pretty village of Halford in the south of the county, where the medieval bridge (now bypassed by a modern replacement) bears battle scars sustained in the Civil War, a stark reminder that Cavaliers and Roundheads realised the strategic value of the old Roman road.

Not far away lies Tredington (*inset*), often described as 'the archetypal English village', where the needle spire of the parish church of St Gregory is a familiar landmark for miles around. The church, dating from Saxon times, contains a wealth of interest for visitors, including, curiously, the remains of 10th-century doors set high in the old stone walls. Their seemingly inaccessible position is accounted for by the fact that the villagers in those early days would have entered the church by means of ladders, which could then be pulled up after them to afford protection from the marauding Danes.

As it makes its almost unwavering way across the county, the Fosse Way encounters not a single town, leaving its delightfully rural character unchallenged. Shipston-on-Stour is bypassed to its east, and Leamington Spa to its west, while Coventry and Rugby are left almost equidistant on either side. It's not until it crosses the county boundary and arrives at Roman Leicester that an urban environment confronts it. But that's another story.

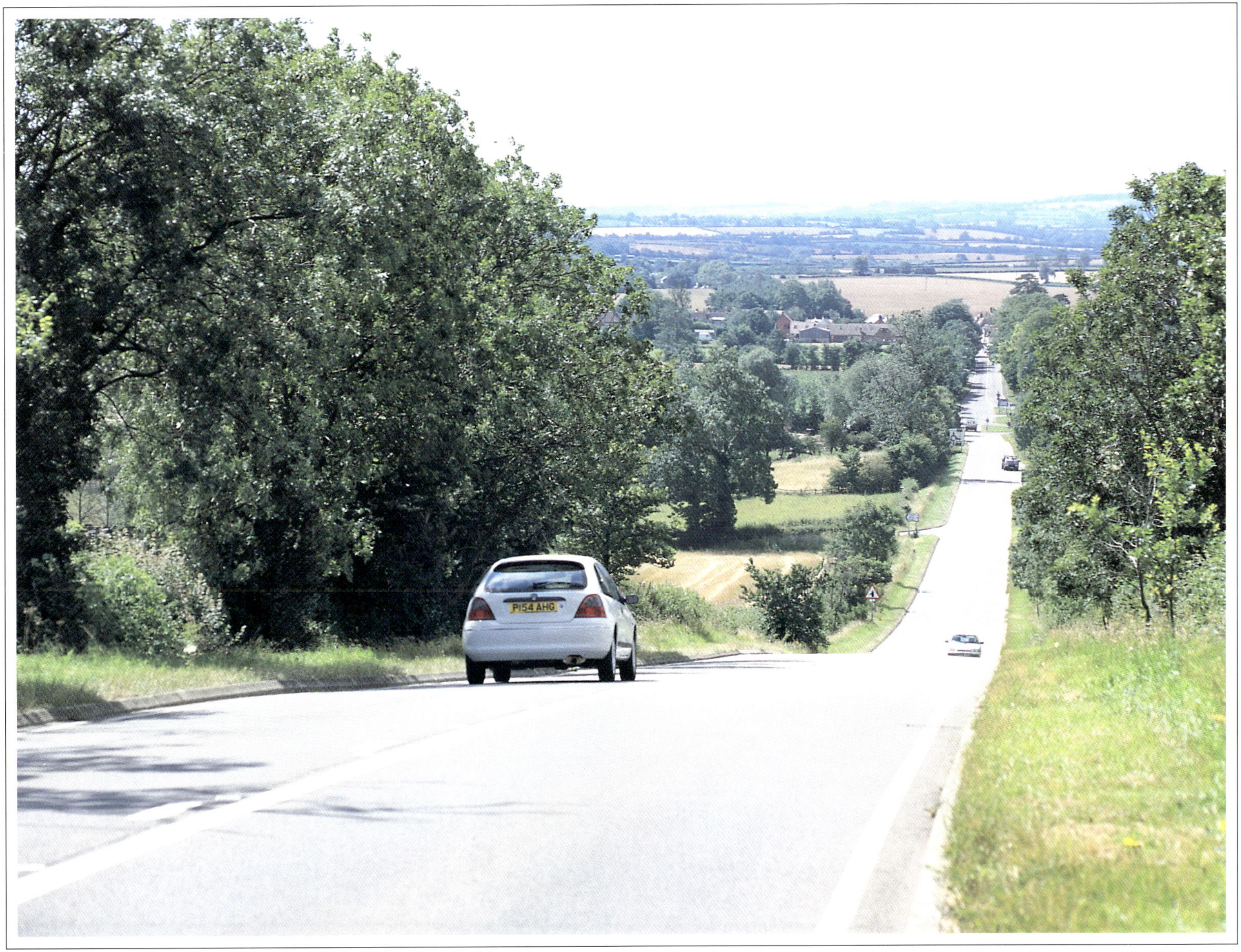
P154 AHG

Kineton and Edgehill

There's a fine line to be drawn between a small town and a large village. Kineton, in the eyes of the outsider at least, tends to sit right on that line, as it could quite easily fall into either category. But to the locals, regardless of its size, Kineton indisputably is a village.

At its heart stands the golden-stone medieval church of St Peter, its sturdy tower looking out over a fair scene which has managed to escape most of the worst excesses of 20th-century planners. The old streets are lined with a pleasing medley of buildings (*opposite*), and the Market Square survives as a reminder of the long-gone days when Kineton had its own regular cattle market. Indeed, one explanation of Kineton's name is that it is derived from *Kine* (or cattle) town. Another attributes it to *King* town, as it was a royal manor in Anglo-Saxon times, being called Kington in the Domesday Survey.

Kineton's long history is also apparent in the remains by the little river Dene of a substantial motte-and-bailey castle, a fortification popularly named after King John who is said to have held a court here.

More than 400 years later another episode in English history made its mark on Kineton when the Parliamentary forces stayed here prior to the Battle of Edgehill which took place nearby on 23rd October, 1642. The site of this first great battle of the Civil War (*inset*) is still identifiable today. It takes little imagination to visualise the Royalists grouped along the top of the Edgehill escarpment, facing the Parliamentarians down below, and it's whispered hereabouts that on the anniversary of the battle each year, if you listen very intently, you can hear the sounds of the bloody skirmish which ensued.

Certainly, visitors to the Castle Inn at Edgehill can see a collection of armour, pistols and swords dug up on the nearby battlefield, but the battlemented tower which adjoins the inn was not involved in the Civil War at all. Based on Guy's Tower at Warwick Castle, it is said to stand on the spot where the king's standard was raised, and was built to mark the battle's 100th anniversary by the celebrated architect Sanderson Miller, whose home was at nearby Radway Grange.

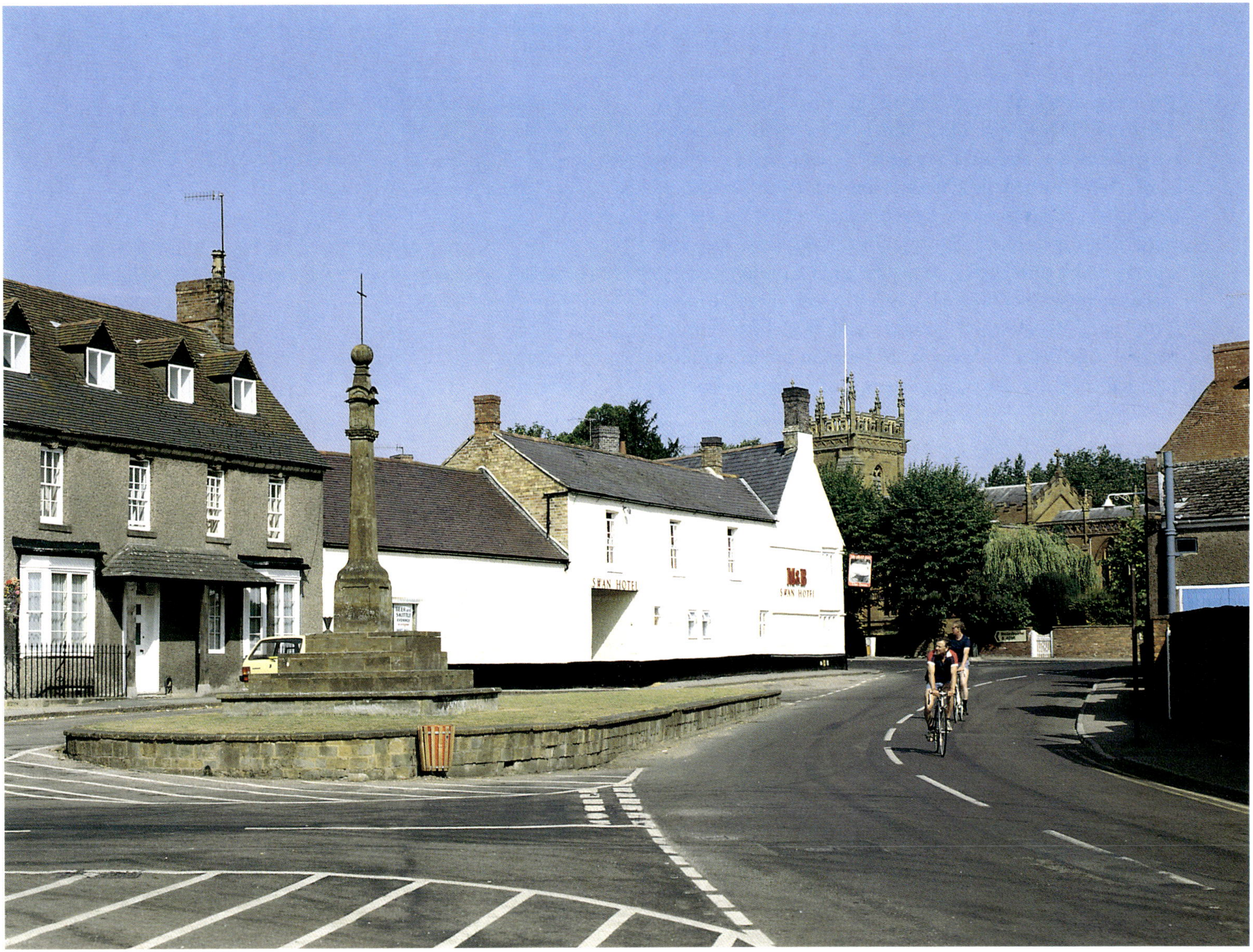
SWAN HOTEL
M&B
SWAN HOTEL

Radway and Warmington

In a county where hills worthy of their name are relatively few and far between, those which do exist have taken on a significance – almost a reverence – which they would hardly have earned in Cumbria or the Peak District of Derbyshire. Thus the lofty Edgehill escarpment has lent its name to its immediate surroundings which have become known, albeit unofficially, as the Edgehill Country.

Ratley, perched 600 feet up on the escarpment's eastern flank, with its thatched cottages and fine 14th-century church of St Peter ad Vincula (St Peter in bonds), typifies the charm of the Edgehill villages, but it cannot boast a mansion as splendid as Radway Grange – pictured (*opposite*) across a snowy landscape – which stands close to Radway village on the other side of the hill.

The village itself, with its broach-spired Victorian church dedicated to St Peter (this time, not in bonds) and its old stone cottages, possesses its own distinctive character, but it is the impressive Grange which adds that extra touch of quality. Set in spacious parkland, it can claim Elizabethan origins, although it has been substantially altered during its long life, notably by the celebrated Warwickshire architect Sanderson Miller, who lived here in the 18th century. Another celebrated owner was Field Marshal Earl Haig, who journeyed from his Radway home in the First World War to become Commander-in-Chief of the British forces at Flanders.

Not far from Radway lies Warmington, a pretty village clinging snugly to Edgehill's eastern slopes. It nudges a steep gradient on the once busy trunk road linking Warwick and Banbury which, mercifully, has now lost at least some of its traffic to the nearby M40 motorway. By the side of the main road stands the church of St Michael where, in its sloping churchyard, lie buried just a few of the hapless soldiers slain at the Battle of Edgehill. From here, a narrow lane descends into Warmington itself, to reveal a vista which confirms the village's reputation as one of the showplaces of rural Warwickshire (*inset*).

The gabled manor house of around 1600, the elegant Georgian former rectory, and a delightful variety of Hornton stone cottages are grouped around a triangular green and picture-book pond, a scene immortalised by countless photographers and artists over the years.

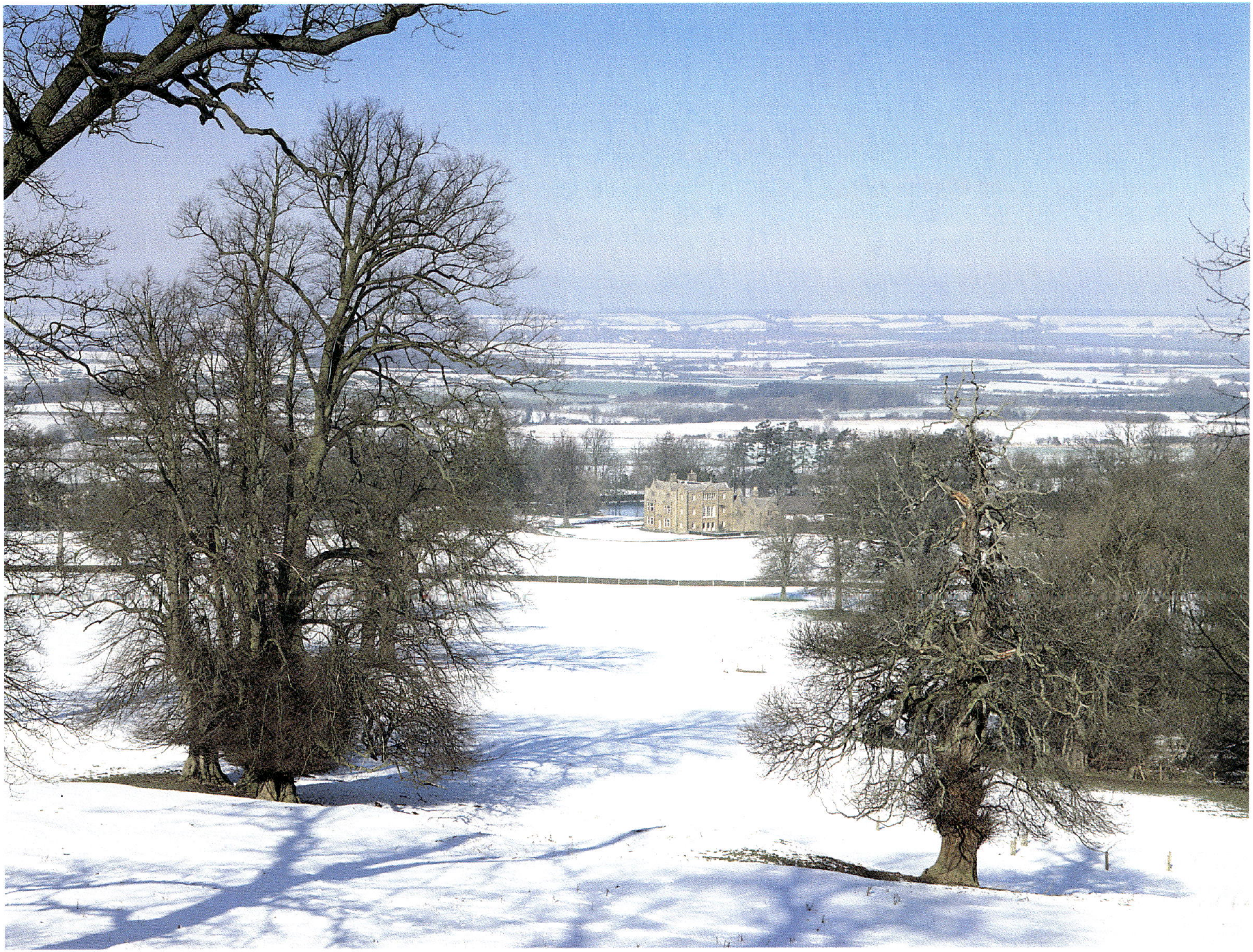

The Burton Dassett Hills

Focal point of a popular country park, the gentle humps of the Burton Dassett Hills today attract leisure-seekers in their hundreds, who come here to walk, to picnic, to ride their ponies and to fly their kites on the windy slopes. The hills are also a mecca for amateur fossil-hunters attracted by the spoils of the long-gone quarrymen who once made a living from the iron-rich, golden-brown sandstone.

Crowning the hills is an ancient stone beacon tower (*opposite*) erected in the early 16th century by Sir Edward Belknap, a ruthless absentee landlord responsible for depopulating local communities in order to gain grazing land for his sheep. It was a fiery beacon from this tower which transmitted to London, via a chain of similar beacons, news of the Royalist victory at Edgehill during the Civil War. Until 1946 a windmill shared the hilltop with the beacon tower, but it was blown down in a storm and never replaced.

The village of Burton Dassett, once large enough to hold its own market, was one of Belknap's targets for depopulation, and all that remains today is little more than the Norman church, the Victorian Grecian-style Holy Well, a farmhouse and the old vicarage. The church, architecturally and decoratively, is among the finest in Warwickshire, one of its more unusual features being the gradual stepping of the floor to allow for the sloping land on which it was built.

Dotted around the hills there are other pleasant villages too, like Northend and Knightcote, Fenny Compton and Avon Dassett, and the more modern Temple Herdewyke, cheek-by-jowl with the vast army depot which it largely serves.

Farnborough, a little further south, is a historic village familiar to stately-home devotees who come here to visit Farnborough Hall (*inset*), the impressive seat of the Holbech family. Set in magnificent landscaped grounds which include lakes, temples and a broad elevated terrace with fine panoramic views, the classical mansion dates mainly from the mid-18th century and now belongs to the National Trust.

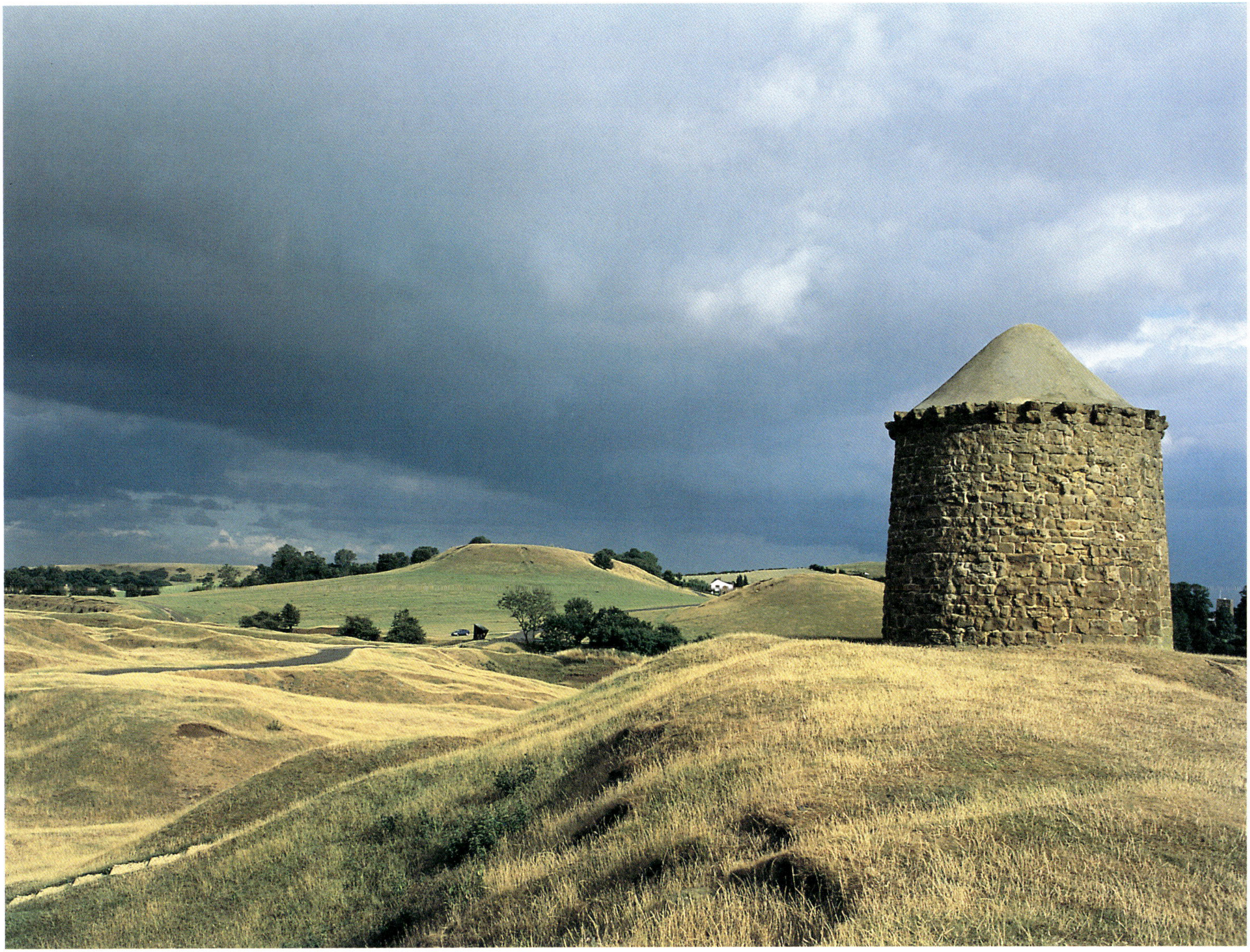

Tysoe and Upton House

Tysoe is, in fact, three separate communities, close to the Oxfordshire border to the north-east of Shipston-on-Stour. The unusual name alludes to the Saxon war-god Tiw, who has also given his name to *Tuesday*. Tysoe thus means 'the land of Tiw', an explanation which always guarantees an appreciative nod from those with an interest in place-names. Tiw's trusty steed is said to have been the inspiration for the outline of a giant horse cut into the red soil of a nearby hillside, which, although long disappeared, is recalled in a local name still used in the area, the Vale of the Red Horse.

Lower Tysoe, the most northerly of the trio of villages, was once known as Temple Tysoe, reflecting the fact that its land belonged to the Knights Templar who were based at Balsall (now Temple Balsall) between Knowle and Coventry. A few hundred yards to the south lie Middle and Upper Tysoe, contiguous communities which together form the main centre of population.

A Norman church, the popular Peacock Inn, a modern Methodist church, a sprinkling of shops, a school and a diminutive fire station confer a certain status on Middle Tysoe (*inset*), while the village is also the home of a remarkable cottage industry which has grown over the years into something of a national institution. This is the bakery of Meg Rivers, whose home-made cakes are now mailed to thousands of devotees all over the country as well as overseas.

Just to the south of the Tysoes, nestling picturesquely in a hollow, is Compton Wynyates, widely acknowledged as one of the most perfect Tudor mansions in England. Sadly, this beautiful house is no longer open to the public, but a few miles to the north another grand edifice welcomes visitors in their thousands. This is Upton House (*opposite*), an impressive building of mellow local stone, now a National Trust property, noted for its outstanding collections of paintings and porcelain assembled by the second Lord Bearsted.

The collections include many important works by major English and continental artists, Brussels tapestries, Chelsea figures, Sevres porcelain and rare furniture, much of it from the 18th century. The landscaped grounds, home of the national collection of asters, are another of Upton's attractions. They feature steep terracing, a beautiful 1930s water garden, ornamental pools, and an exemplary kitchen garden to inspire even the most self-assured owners of vegetable plots.

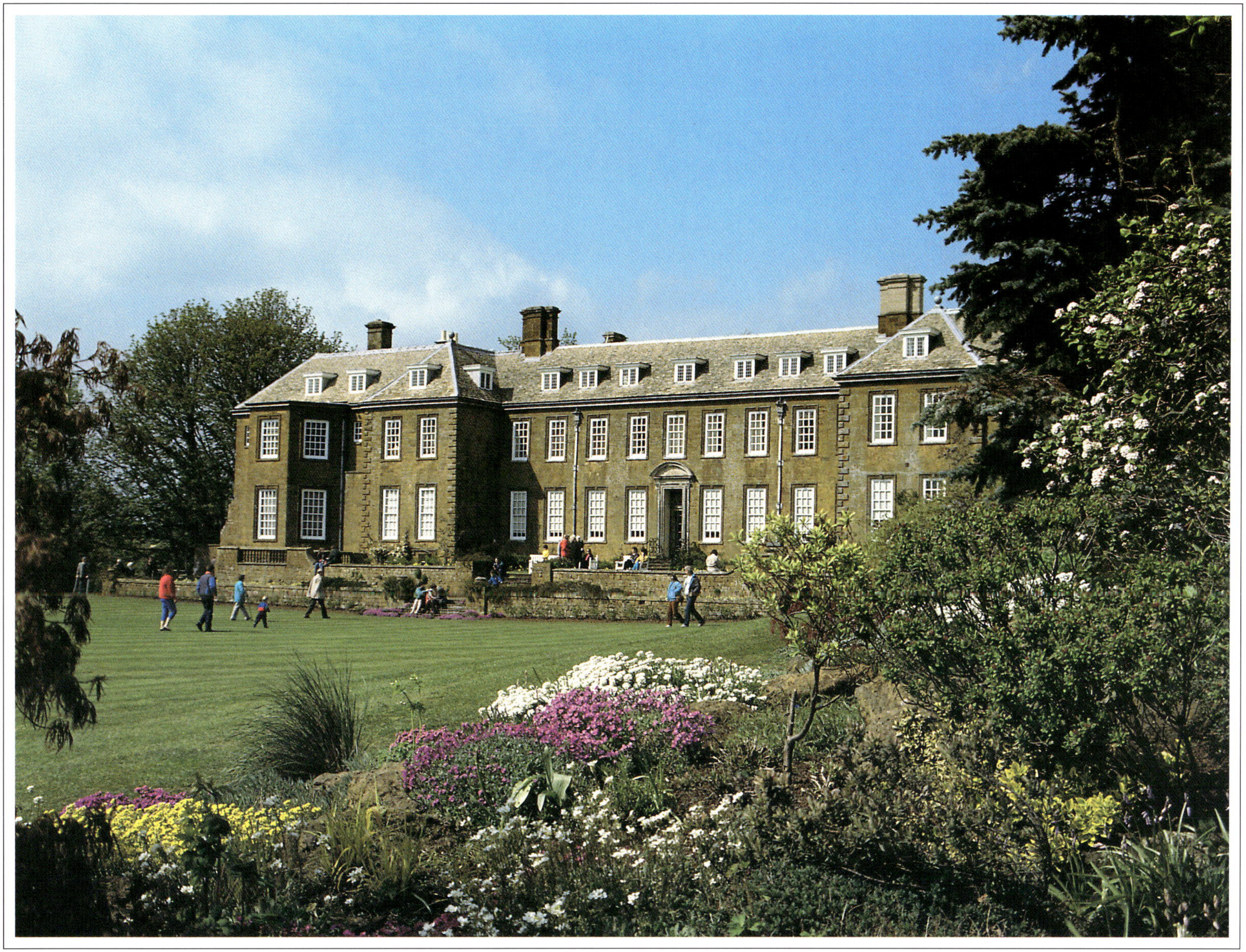

Welford-on-Avon and Bidford-on-Avon

From its source at Naseby in Northamptonshire to its confluence with the Severn at Tewkesbury, the river Avon hosts along its banks a rich diversity of historic towns and villages.

A few miles downstream from Stratford, the river loops round one of the most idyllic of these, Welford-on-Avon, not to be confused with its namesake close to the river's source. Welford has managed to retain much of its traditional charm, although numerous modern dwellings have now sprung up among the stone and brick-and-timber cottages of earlier centuries, many topped by neat thatch (*inset*).

Welford owes its Saxon origins to the monks of Deerhurst Priory in Gloucestershire. The site of their original place of worship is now occupied by the fine Norman church of St Peter, which counts among its treasures a rare Saxon font bowl once used by the monks. An endearing rural custom for which the village is noted is the annual ceremony of dancing round the 65-foot-high red, white and blue maypole on the village green.

Another place with its roots deep in history is Bidford-on-Avon, a little further downstream from Welford. This is the point where the Romans' Ryknild Street forded the river on its way to Alauna, better known today as Alcester, a few miles to the north. The ford was eventually replaced by the present eight-arch medieval bridge (*opposite*) which, having survived partial destruction in the Civil War, now has to contend with the demands of modern traffic trying to negotiate its narrow confines.

Bidford's most notable landmark is the tower of the parish church of St Laurence. The church itself, set in a churchyard stretching down to the river, has undergone many changes over the centuries, notably in Victoria's reign, and is a building of considerable architectural interest.

Overlooking the small village square is the former Falcon Inn, a sturdy gabled building of mellow stone in which Shakespeare is said to have drunk considerably more than was good for him during a drinking contest with local topers. It was an episode recorded for posterity in the well-known quatrain which refers, pointedly, to 'drunken Bidford'. Whether or not Shakespeare wrote it, as is popularly supposed, is an ongoing debate.

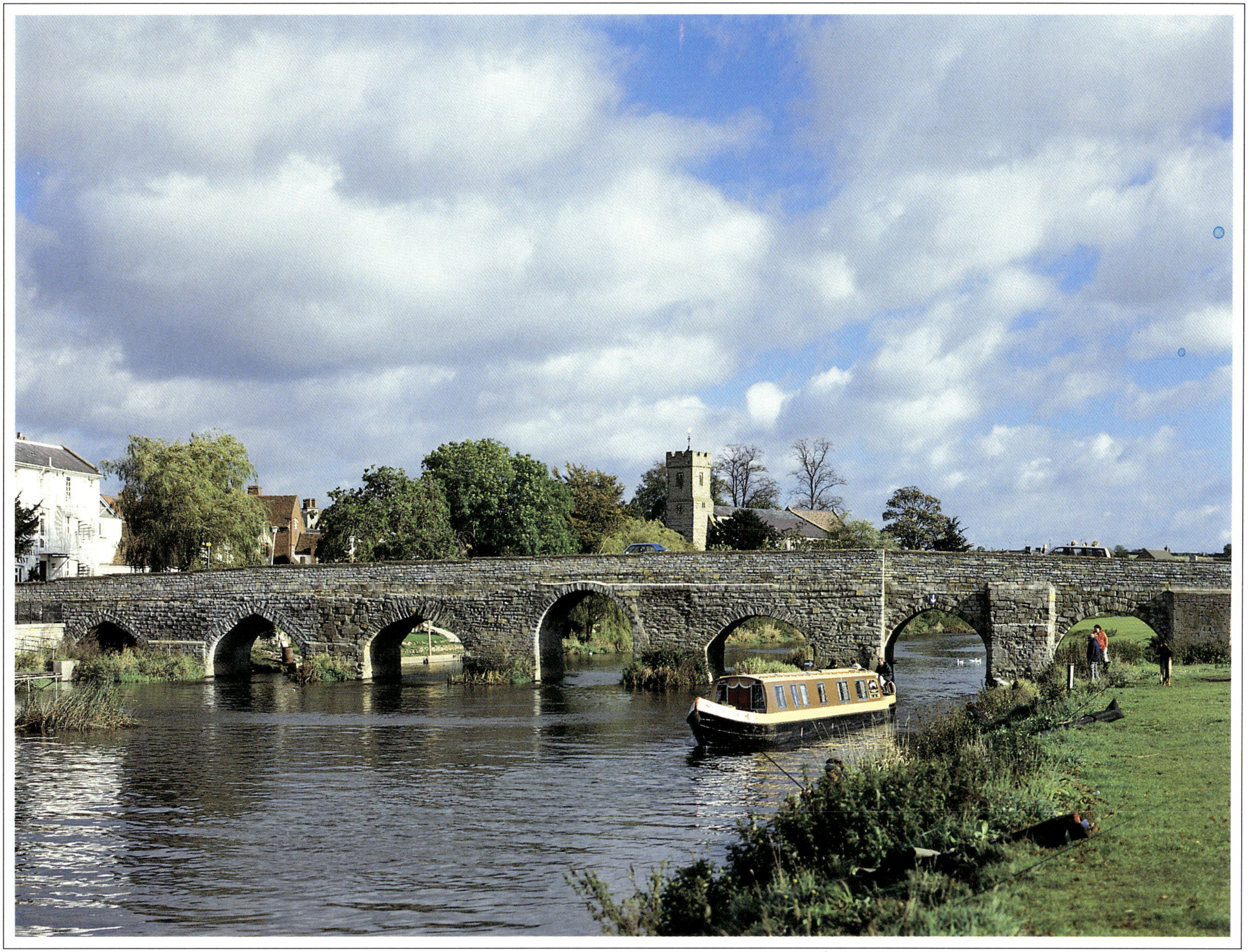

Shakespeare in Trust

To paraphrase the Bard himself, Stratford is a town which has had greatness thrust upon it. Without the influence of Shakespeare, Stratford today would be just another English market town instead of a major cultural mecca for the world's tourists.

Much of the credit for Stratford's relative dignity as a major tourist centre goes to the Shakespeare Birthplace Trust, zealous guardians of the principal Shakespearian properties. It operates from the surprisingly modern Shakespeare Centre, right next door to Shakespeare's Birthplace in Henley Street (*opposite*), a revered shrine visited by tens of thousands of people each year.

Another Trust property is Nash's House, once the home of Thomas Nash, first husband of Shakespeare's granddaughter Elizabeth, adjoining the now landscaped site of New Place where Shakespeare spent his retirement. It was a subsequent owner of New Place, the Reverend Francis Gastrell, who saw fit to demolish it in 1759, an act of vandalism which he justified on the grounds that the building's large numbers of sightseers were becoming a nuisance.

The third of the Trust's Stratford properties is timber-framed Hall's Croft, formerly the home of Dr John Hall, the local physician who married Shakespeare's elder daughter Susanna. One of its rooms has been furnished as an authentic Elizabethan dispensary.

The Shakespeare Birthplace Trust also administers Anne Hathaway's Cottage at nearby Shottery (*inset*), where Shakespeare courted the daughter of Richard Hathaway before their marriage in 1582; and Mary Arden's House in the village of Wilmcote. This was once the home of Shakespeare's mother, who set out from here in 1557 to marry John Shakespeare, and produced a son who was to become the greatest playwright in the world.

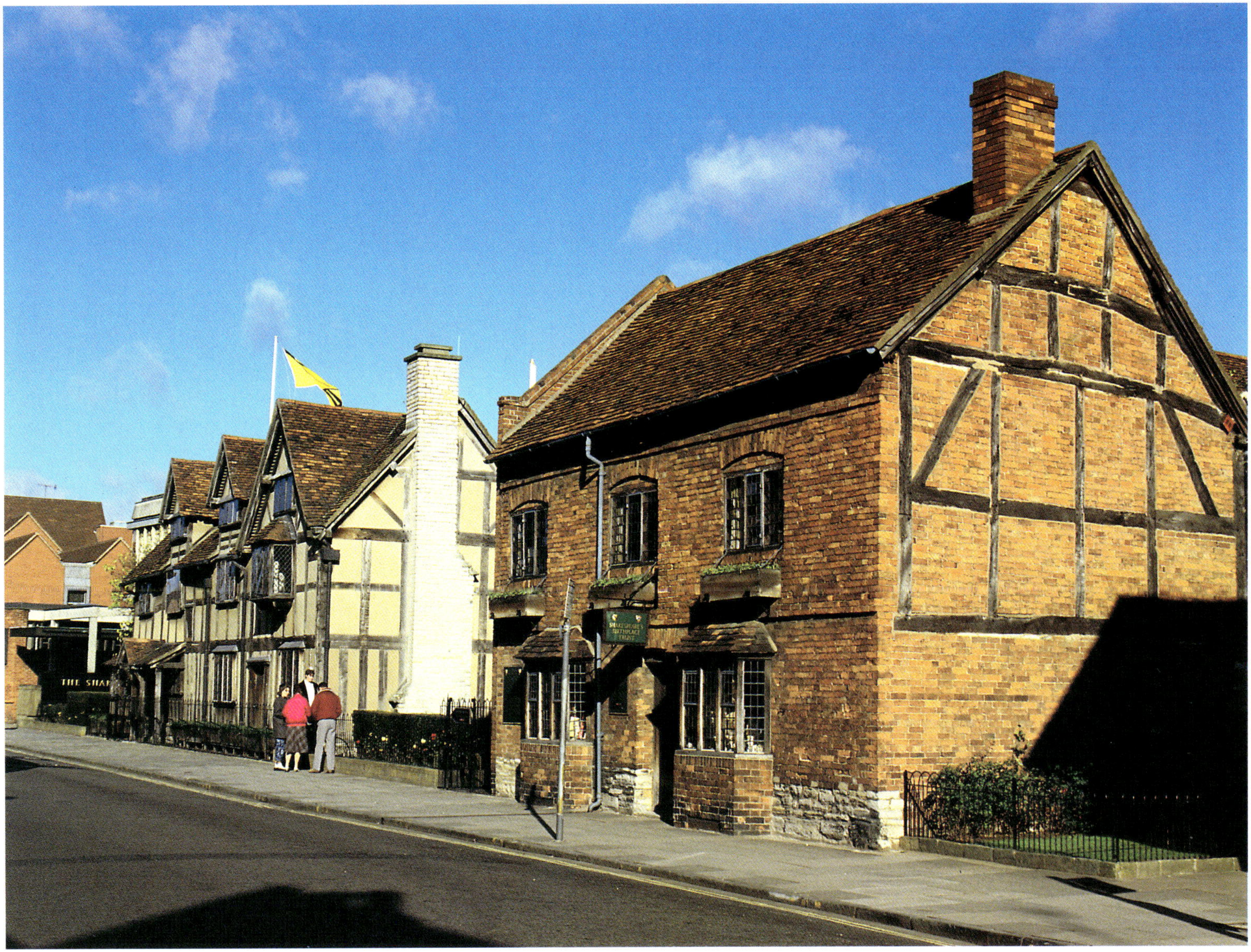

Stratford-upon-Avon

If you go to Stratford with a wish to ignore Shakespeare, it's virtually impossible to do so. Even disregarding the important Shakespearian properties described on the previous page, you cannot go far in the town without encountering a building or other landmark associated in one way or another with the Bard.

Almost too obvious to single out is the world-renowned Royal Shakespeare Theatre (*opposite*), built in 1932 on the banks of the Avon after fire gutted its predecessor. Linked to it in a surviving part of the original building is the Swan Theatre, and close by stands The Other Place, completing the Royal Shakespeare Company's remarkable trio of theatres in which the plays of Shakespeare and his contemporaries are regularly performed. Four of Shakespeare's principal characters – Hamlet (*inset*), Prince Henry, Falstaff and Lady Macbeth – are commemorated on Lord Ronald Gower's statue of the Bard in the colourful Bancroft Gardens.

Nearby, linking the Avon to the restored Stratford Canal, is the town's picturesque canal basin, now the haunt of leisure-seekers but still a reminder of an important era in local commercial history. Another such reminder is the old red-brick bridge over the Avon which once carried a horse-tramway to Moreton-in-Marsh; it is close to Stratford's famous Clopton Bridge, given to the town in the late 15th century by a local benefactor, Sir Hugh Clopton, who became Lord Mayor of London.

A short distance downstream stands Holy Trinity church where Shakespeare lies buried. This, not surprisingly, is another of the town's principal places of pilgrimage.

There is no other small town in England which offers such a wealth of interest packed into a mere handful of streets. The ancient Guild Chapel, built for the Guild of the Holy Cross, formerly the town's ruling body, is one focus of attention. Visitors from the United States make a beeline for ornate Harvard House, which has associations with John Harvard who founded the American university. Even many of the town's well-patronised hotels are historical attractions in their own right, like the Shakespeare, a stunning example of Tudor timbering, or the mellow brick Alveston Manor, in whose grounds the first performance of *A Midsummer Night's Dream* is popularly said to have taken place. There's the Falcon, too, whose ancient timbers date back to around 1500.

Despite all the pressures that tourism can bring, Stratford still manages to remain a workaday Warwickshire market town. It's just that Shakespeare has given it a status which is unique.

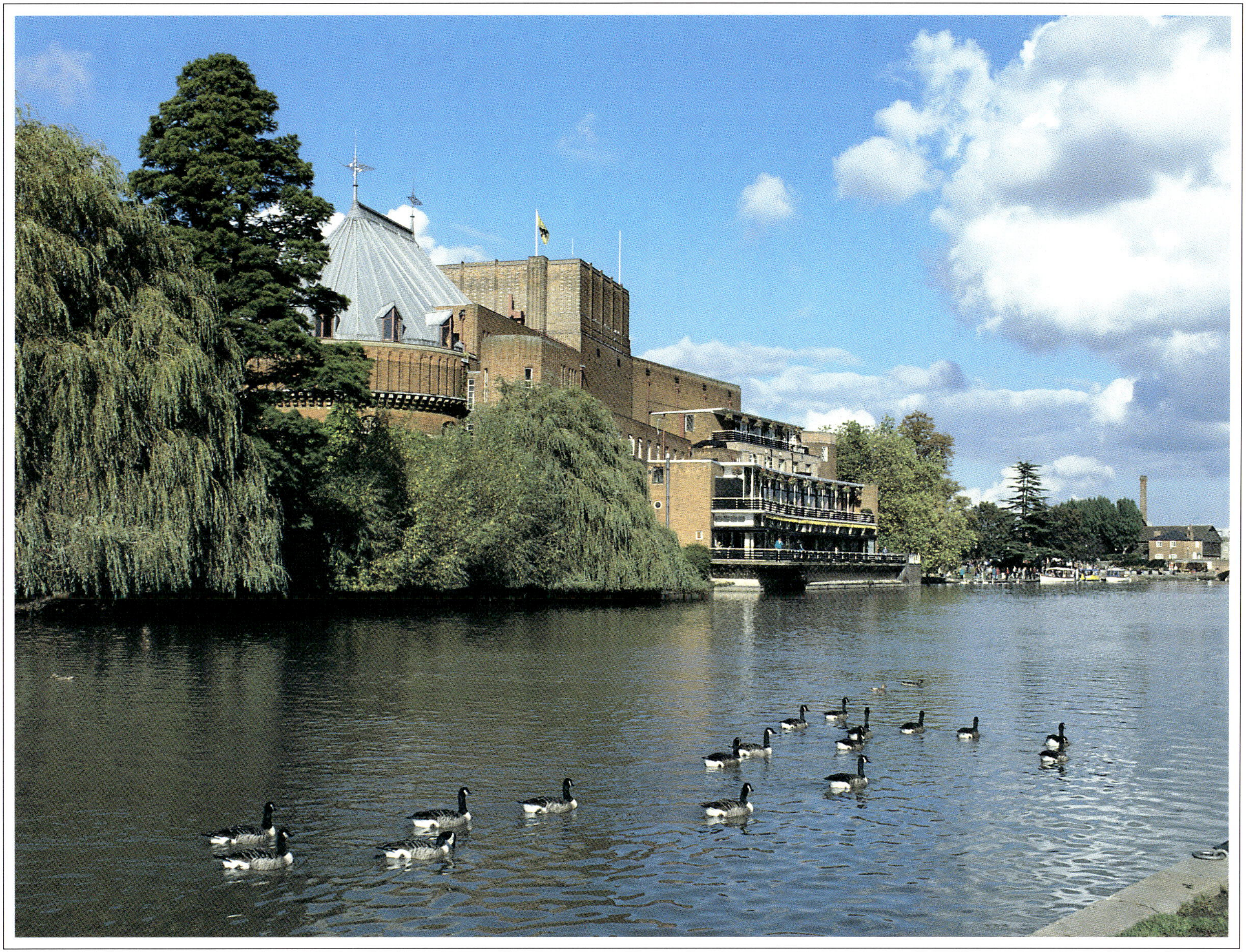

Alcester

For the Romans, Alcester was a town of considerable regional importance, standing as it does on their vital transport artery, Ryknild Street, at the confluence of the rivers Alne and Arrow, surrounded by fertile farmland.

With geographical and historical credentials like that, Alcester was seemingly ripe for development over the centuries into a sizeable centre of population and commerce, like Chester or York or any other city with Roman roots. But it was not to be; Alcester somehow escaped the inexorable march of urban progress, and it has never outgrown its modest status as a small market town.

Today, Alcester's intrinsic charm has largely survived intact without being marred by the high-rise tower blocks, the multi-storey car parks and the more obtrusive results of 20th-century development which have afflicted so many other places. A much-needed bypass has relieved the town centre of most its former traffic congestion, and any industrial development has been largely confined to its own purpose-built estate on the outskirts.

Dominated by the handsome parish church of St Nicholas, the gently curving High Street, pictured (*opposite*) from the churchyard, has changed little over the centuries, apart from cosmetic alterations to some of the old buildings, and its shops not only serve the town itself, but a wide surrounding rural area. Sadly for those with a sweet tooth, the town can no longer boast the surfeit of bakeries (there were once 13 in the High Street alone) which earned Alcester the sobriquet of Caketown.

Because the developers have, on the whole, been kind to Alcester, many of its finer architectural legacies survive, including a wealth of eye-catching timbered properties typified by those which line picturesque Malt Mill Lane. The early 17th-century islanded Town Hall building, bordered by quaintly narrow Butter Street, is another notable local landmark, in stark architectural contrast to the former Victorian needle factory which stands as an evocative reminder of a once important local industry.

Alcester, understandably, attracts its fair share of visitors, many of whom know the town for its proximity to two of the Midlands' most impressive stately homes. Coughton Court, ancestral home of the Throckmorton family, lies a couple of miles to the north, and Ragley Hall, seat of the ninth Marquess of Hertford in its magnificent parkland, stands close to the pretty hamlet of Arrow (*inset*), a similar distance to the south.

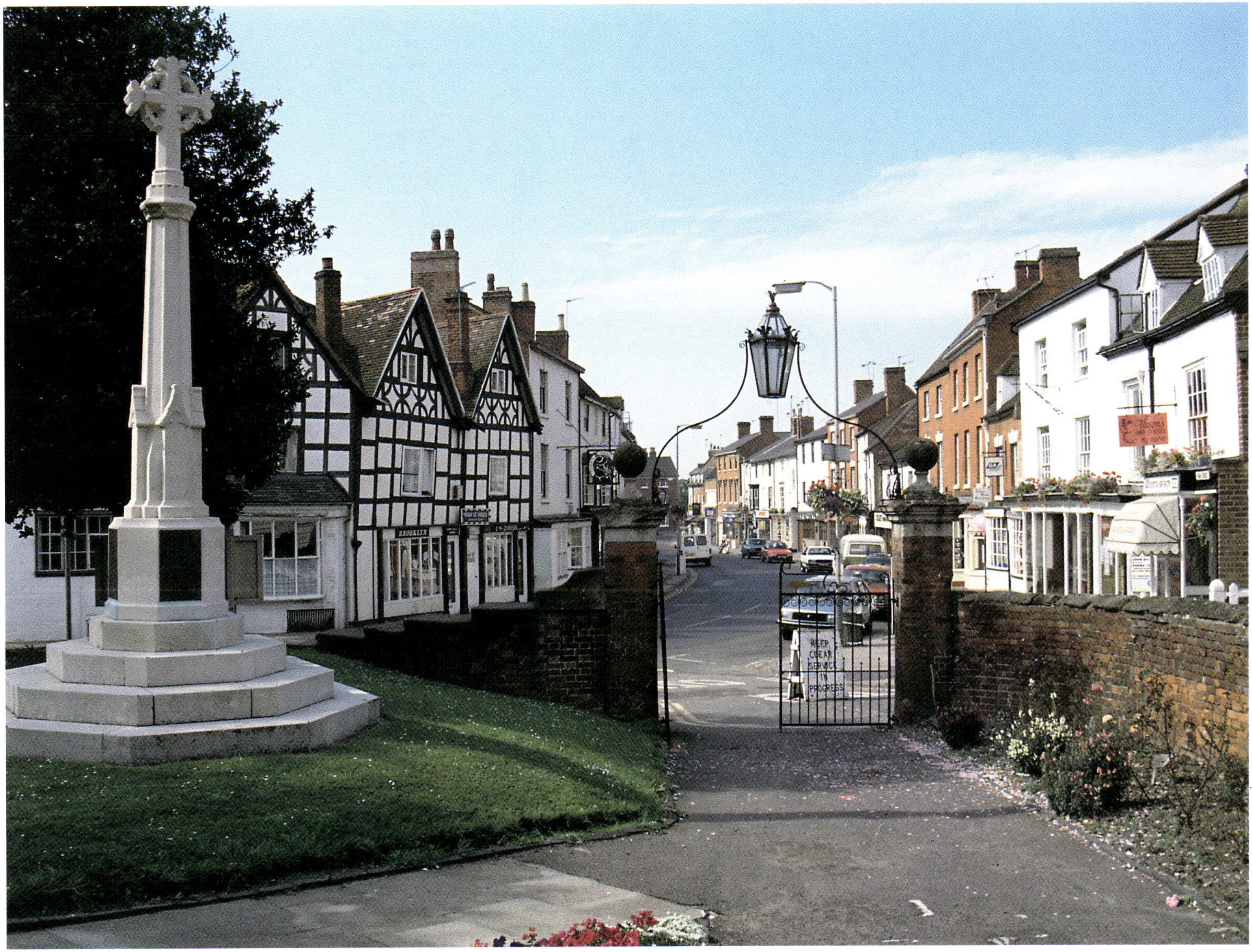

Henley-in-Arden

Like Alcester, Henley-in-Arden is a modest little market town which has never been allowed to outgrow itself. It, too, has a long history, and its name is a reminder of the days when the great Forest of Arden flourished all around. Henley's origins date back to the time when it was a settlement under the protection of the de Montforts, the Norman overlords whose motte-and-bailey castle once dominated the hill across the river Alne to the east. Surviving evidence of the castle's earthworks can still be seen to this day.

The town's High Street, almost a mile long, has managed to retain its considerable charm, despite the fact that it is part of the busy Stratford to Birmingham road (*opposite*). Dominating the halfway point is the sturdy tower of the 15th-century church of St John the Baptist, adjoining the old timber-framed Guildhall in which the town's historic Court Leet still meets.

Less than a quarter of mile from the church of St John, across the river Alne, stands the Norman church of St Nicholas at Beaudesert (*inset*), historically a separate community but today essentially a part of Henley. Rarely can two Anglican parish churches be found in such close proximity.

But ecclesiastical niceties apart, it's Henley's attractive High Street for which the town is principally known. Bordered by a rich assortment of buildings of mellow stone, brick and timbering, it is enhanced by numerous old inns, some still proudly exhibiting evidence of their coaching origins in the days when the town was on one of the busiest stagecoach routes in the Midlands.

A reminder of Henley's long history as an important market town is the old market cross which stands in the High Street overlooked by the classical façade of Stone House. No longer, though, does it witness the busy activities of the market traders who once gathered here to sell their wares. Henley's market, as popular and vibrant as ever, now flourishes on another site.

Henley, like all Warwickshire towns, has not been immune to expansion, and it has seen the arrival of many modern housing developments, especially in recent years. But in deference to the architectural heritage which lends the town so much of its character, the planners have ensured that most of the new building has taken place around the periphery, leaving the historic heart visually intact.

HENLEY
ICE CREAM
Ye Olde Tudor Dairies
SCHOOL ROAD
HENLEY
ICE CREAM
ON SALE HERE

Barford

The Trade Union movement owes a debt of gratitude to a resident of Barford who was born in a tiny cottage opposite the church in 1826 and died there in 1919. He was Joseph Arch, an agricultural worker who decided that the pittance he and his fellow workers were receiving for their labours was grossly unfair. He organised a protest meeting in the neighbouring village of Wellesbourne for the purpose of establishing a union of farmworkers.

The date was 7th February 1872, and the outcome of the meeting was the formation of a trade union for the farmworkers of Warwickshire. This eventually blossomed into the National Agricultural Labourers' Union, the first-ever body of its kind to represent the interests of those who earned a living off the land. Arch had made his point, and he went on to become a Liberal Member of Parliament.

Joseph Arch's cottage (*inset*) still stands in Barford, and his grave in the churchyard has become something of a shrine for the farmworkers of today. One of the village's two inns honoured his memory in 1960 when it changed its name from the Red Lion to the Joseph Arch.

If he were to return to Barford today, Arch would hardly recognise parts of the village, although much of it is still as he would have known it. St Peter's church, largely rebuilt during Arch's early life, still serves the village, its 14th-century tower no less of a local landmark today than it was then. The classical rectory next door has now been converted into a popular hotel, and many of the old cottages – and the grander Georgian and Regency houses – which have traditionally contributed to Barford's charm still survive, even though the village has expanded considerably since Arch's day.

Another Barford landmark he would recognise is the fine 18th-century stone bridge (*opposite*) which carries the Warwick to Wellesbourne road over the Avon at the site of an earlier ford. From this peaceful spot it is still possible to look out over the watermeadows towards the tall Victorian spire of All Saints' church in the neighbouring village of Sherbourne, and to see rural Warwickshire at its most serene. It is a scene which Joseph Arch would have known well.

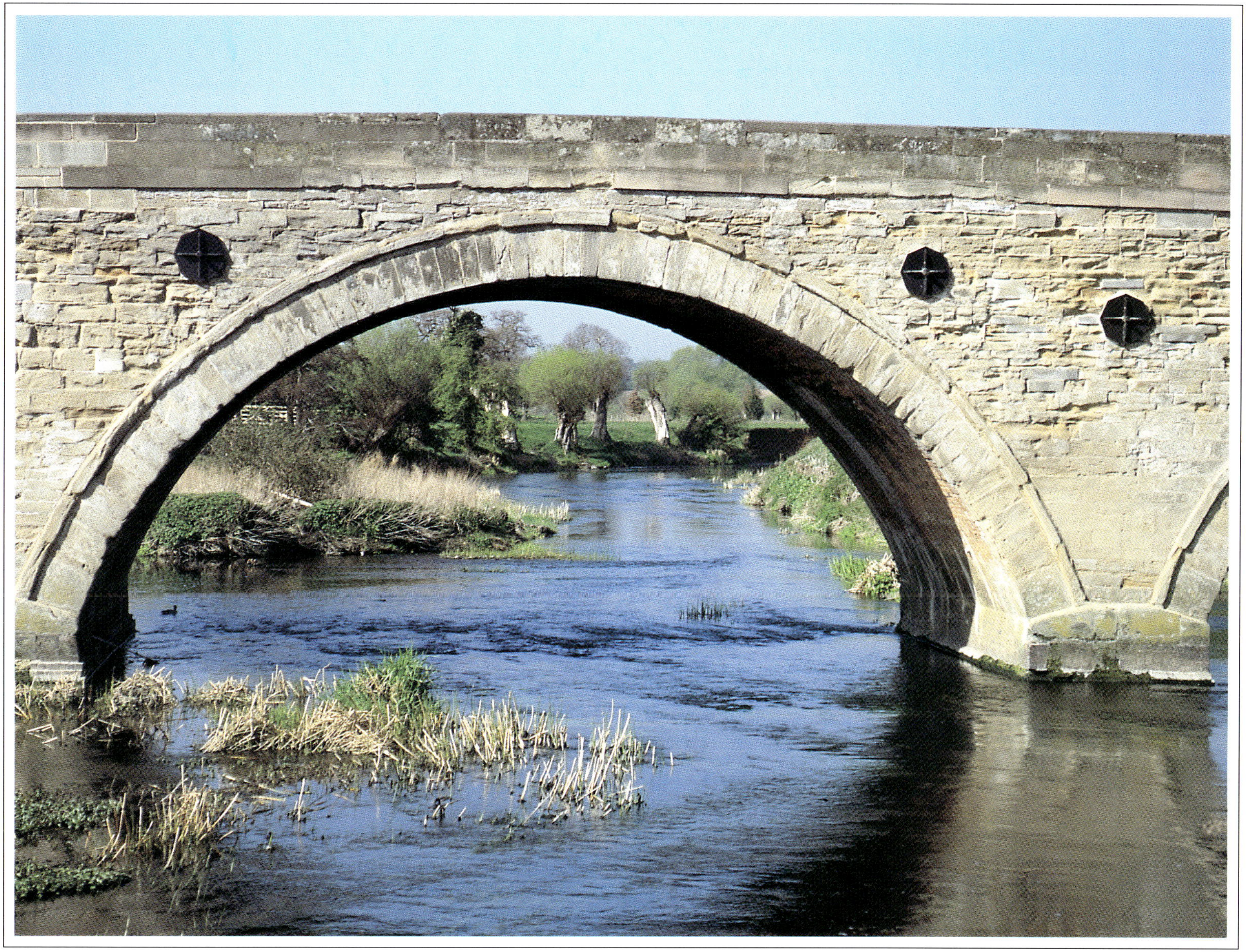

Warwick

When Sir Walter Scott visited Warwick in 1828 and viewed the famous castle by the Avon, he declared that it was 'the most noble sight in all England'. If he were to return today, he could make a similar claim and few would disagree. Generally regarded as the finest medieval castle in England, it ranks among the country's top tourist attractions, welcoming hundreds of thousands of visitors every year from all over the world. For centuries the seat of the Earls of Warwick, the castle (*opposite*) was bought in 1978 by Madame Tussaud's of waxworks fame, and although purist historians may have deplored the sale, at least the great building has every care lavished upon it, so that not only its fabric but its unique heritage are painstakingly preserved.

The castle is, without doubt, Warwick's most notable landmark, and because of this it tends to overshadow the many other delights which the county town has to offer. In 1694, Warwick was devastated by a great fire which consumed many of the timber-framed buildings within the old town walls, as well as much of the famous collegiate church of St Mary (*inset*) which was largely rebuilt. Today, its 175-foot-high tower is a commanding landmark for many miles around, giving the appearance of a great cathedral rather than a parish church. One of its principal treasures is the richly decorated Beauchamp Chapel, reputed to be the finest chantry chapel in England.

As a result of the fire, most of Warwick's finest buildings – and there are many – are 18th-century or later, although there are a few notable exceptions like the timber-framed Lord Leycester Hospital nestling against the chapel-topped stone archway of the town's original West Gate.

Known also today for its famous public school, its racecourse and its traditional street fairs, Warwick – in particular its historic centre – has managed better than many towns to cope with modern-day pressures without sacrificing too much of its traditional character.

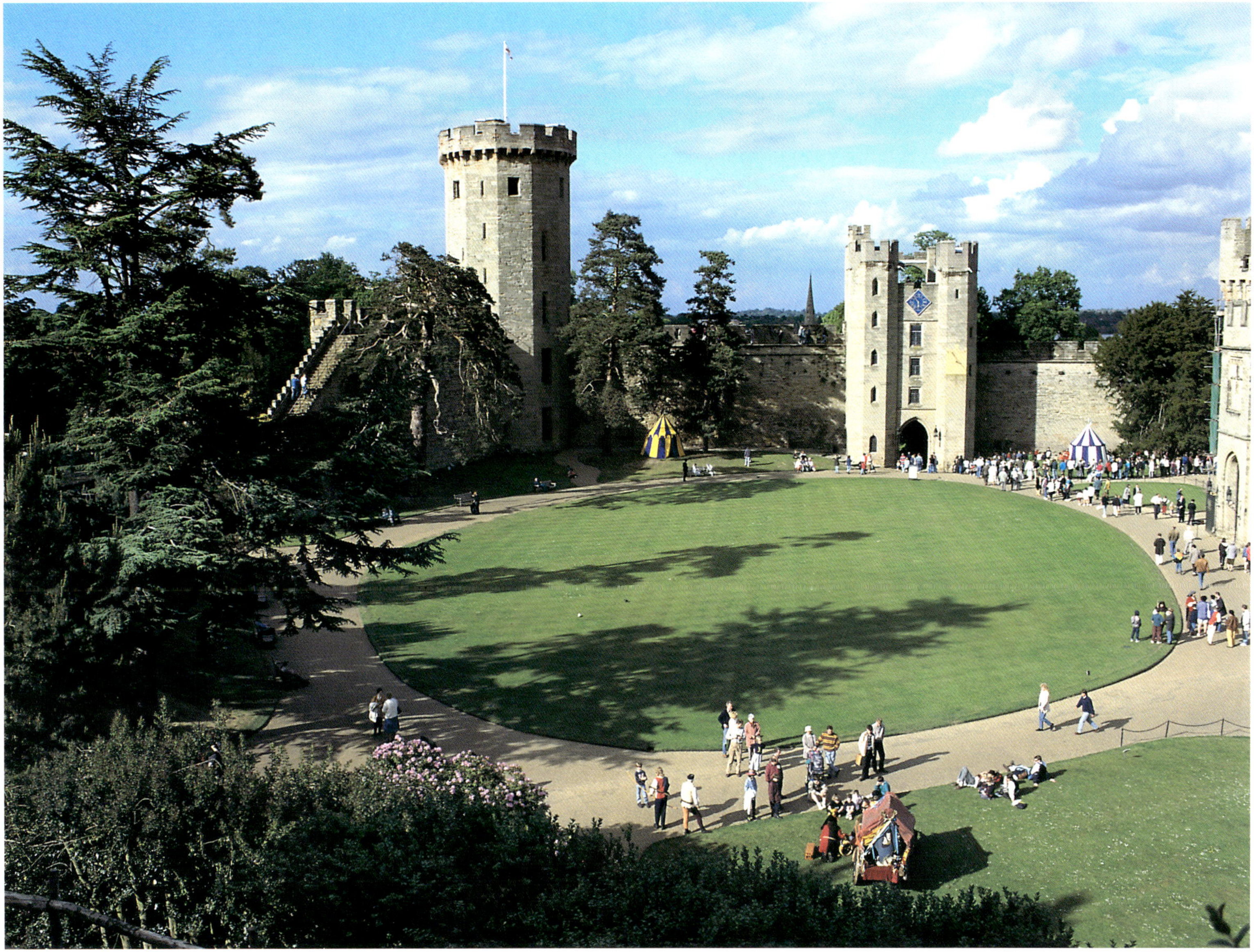

Kenilworth

Those who do not know Kenilworth well could be forgiven for thinking that the town consists of little more than its famous castle and a long shop-lined street – Warwick Road – bounded at one end by the lofty russet-stone church of St John, and at the other by an islanded clock tower.

To passing travellers, this is indeed the impression that Kenilworth offers, which is a pity because if they were to venture off that busy Warwick Road they would discover the older heart of Kenilworth, centred on its short tree-lined High Street distinguished by a medley of elegant buildings. They would find, too, Little Virginia, a picturesque group of timbered and thatched cottages so named because this was where Sir Walter Raleigh is supposed to have planted Virginian potatoes. Another reminder of the old Kenilworth is gently sloping Castle Green with its picturesque cottages (*inset*) and magnificent view of the castle.

Backed by the spacious green expanse of Abbey Fields lies the site of the once influential Kenilworth Abbey, an Augustinian priory founded in the 12th century by Geoffrey de Clinton, chamberlain of Henry I. Not far away, in its leafy setting above the little Finham brook, is the historic parish church of St Nicholas which can count among its many treasures one of the finest Norman doorways in the county.

But Kenilworth, despite its many obvious and less obvious attractions, owes its international fame to the great castle (*opposite*), immortalised as much by the decisive roles it has played in the course of English history, as by Sir Walter Scott's epic novel for which he borrowed the castle's name as a title. In stark contrast to that other great castle in nearby Warwick, Kenilworth's is essentially an impressive ruin, a state it owes to the thorough sacking it received from troops loyal to Cromwell in the 17th century. Yet it still retains evocative reminders of its proud history and its succession of royal owners, even if the great lake which once lapped its western ramparts has long disappeared. It was within the castle's once magnificent interior that Robert Dudley, Earl of Leicester, welcomed Elizabeth I on her various visits, and, according to Scott, had his amorous proposals firmly rejected.

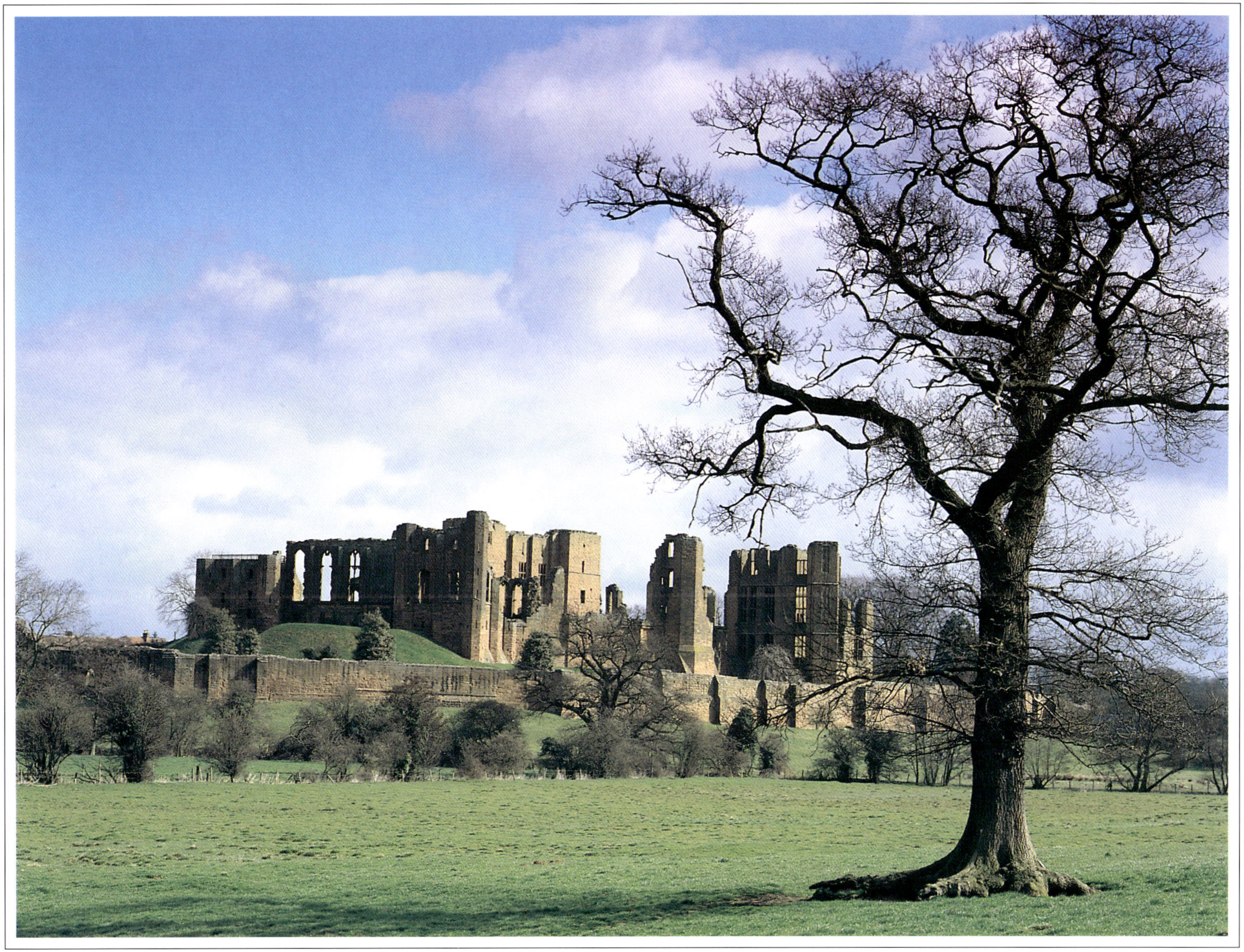

Leamington Spa

The curative waters on which Leamington's fame is founded were first discovered in Tudor times, when the place was no more than a small village by the little river Leam owned by the priors of Kenilworth Abbey, a fact which gave it the name of Leamington Priors. It was not until the late 18th century that the medical (and commercial) potential of the waters began to be realised, and Leamington's destiny was sealed. The town's golden age was during the 19th century when it rapidly developed into a thriving and popular spa. Town planning was on the grand scale, with broad streets lined by elegant Georgian, Regency and Victorian buildings (*opposite*).

The impressive colonnaded Pump Room was built in 1814, and baths, assembly rooms and hotels sprang up at strategic locations around the town. The aristocracy and the rich and famous descended on Leamington in large numbers, intent upon 'taking the waters' to cure their ills, although many were no doubt suffering from nothing more serious than hypochondria. One of the town's more illustrious visitors in 1838 was Queen Victoria, who marked the occasion by granting Leamington the Royal prefix to its name. It has been universally known as Royal Leamington Spa ever since.

Although Leamington's heyday as a spa has long since passed, it is still a notable inland resort. Arthritic duchesses and retired colonels suffering from gout may no longer be seen in their bath chairs, but there's still an unmistakable air of elegance here. The cathedral-like Victorian-Gothic church of All Saints (its lofty tower was added early in the 20th century) remains a formidable Warwickshire landmark, and the flamboyant Victorian town hall still dominates the more restrained façades of the Parade, now one of the Midlands' most popular shopping thoroughfares.

Notable too are the bold frontages of Euston Place and the nearby Regent Hotel, one of the largest hotels in Europe when it was built in 1819. The grand houses of Newbold Terrace also typify Leamington's elegance, although some have now given way to the functional modern architecture of magistrates' courts and the Royal Spa Centre entertainment complex.

Among Leamington's most appealing legacies from its gracious past are the eye-catching Jephson Gardens (*inset*), named after the redoubtable Dr Henry Jephson, the local medical practitioner who was largely responsible for creating the town's reputation as a major English spa.

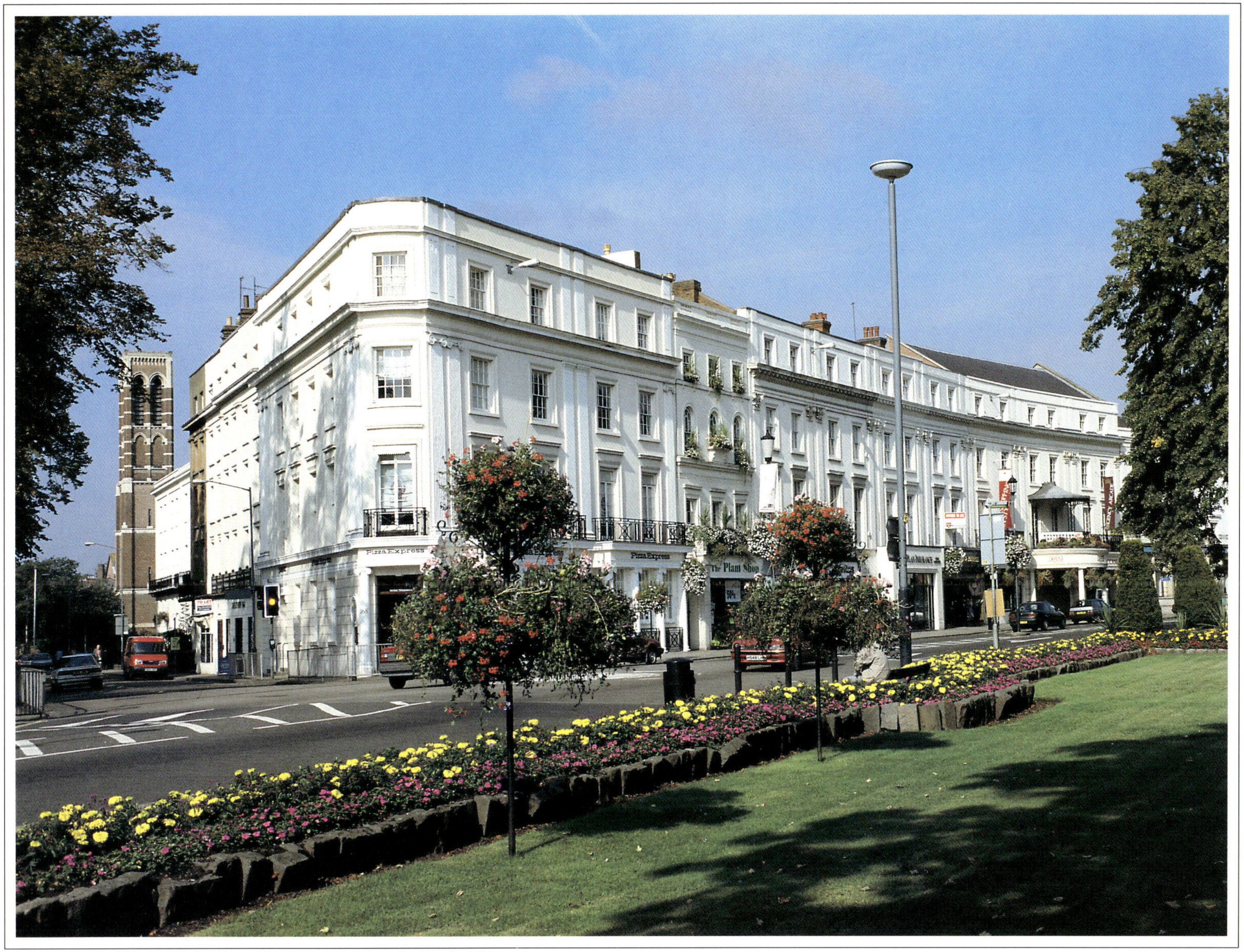
Pizza Express
The Plant Shop

Harbury and Long Itchington

Of all the prehistoric marine reptiles which roamed around these parts 100,000 years ago, one particular ichthyosaurus was destined to put Harbury firmly on the palaeontological map. Its skeleton was discovered in a local quarry and removed to the Natural History Museum in London, where it provided scientists with some revealing research. But prehistoric remains apart, Harbury, a sizeable village a few miles to the south-east of Leamington Spa, has plenty of other reasons to account for its appeal. It's one of those areas which estate agents like to call 'much sought-after', and it can certainly boast some unusual and attractive properties.

One of these, close to the largely 13th-century church of All Saints, is a former place of learning founded in 1611, known as the Wagstaffe School. Another was once a windmill, now without the sails which are said to have killed a former miller. This unfortunate man, so the story goes, is still seen hereabouts in ghostly form, perhaps vying for attention with another of Harbury's ghosts, a mysterious black-coated figure who is occasionally seen hurrying between the old Wagstaffe School and the church.

A local landmark which has dominated the Harbury countryside since 1632 is the famous Chesterton windmill (*opposite*), which stands isolated amid rolling farmland a mile or so to the west. Stone-built on arched pillars and resplendent with restored sails, it is generally assumed to have been the work of the celebrated architect Inigo Jones, although many historians attribute it to Sir Edward Peyto, whose impressive 17th-century mansion once graced the nearby hamlet of Chesterton.

North-east of Harbury, beyond the hamlet of Bascote and across the Grand Union Canal and little river Itchen, lies another of the attractive villages which distinguish this corner of Warwickshire. This is Long Itchington, famed for its picturesque tree-lined pond (*inset*) and its historic Holy Trinity church, parts of which date from the 12th century. The church was once topped by a slender spire, but this collapsed during a storm in 1762, leaving only a stump as a reminder of the sad fate which befell it.

One of Long Itchington's claims to fame is that it was the birthplace of St Wulfstan, Bishop of Worcester in the 11th century, the only Saxon bishop to swear allegiance to William the Conqueror. This timely gesture enabled him to build Worcester's great cathedral, of which his crypt remains an architectural treasure to this day.

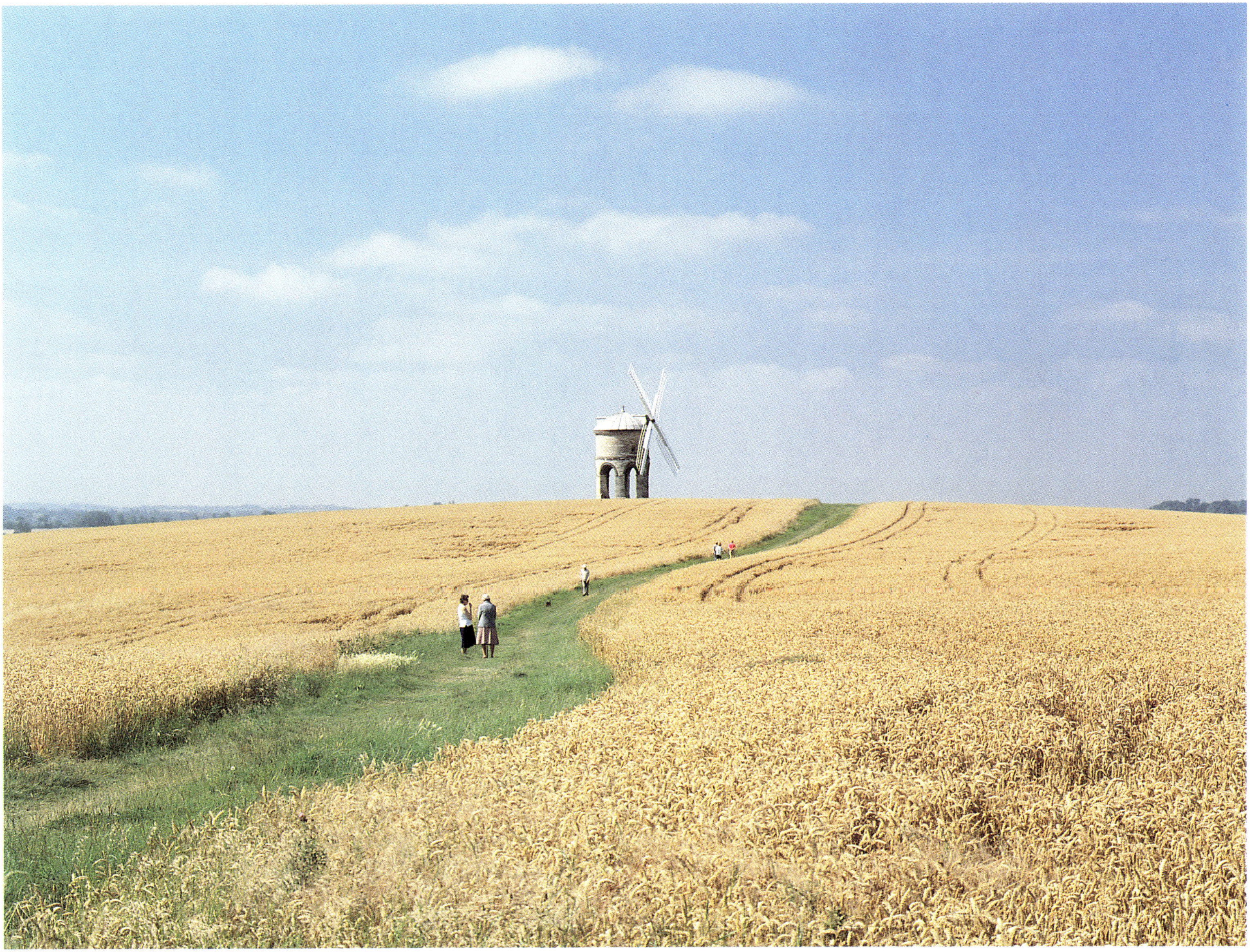

Southam

Until the Second World War, Southam grew very little and remained a small and sleepy town with a close-knit community which lived its day-to-day life much as it had done for centuries. But the age of the motor car soon made an impact on the town, which started to attract large numbers of outsiders keen to settle in a place that was still essentially rural in character, yet within easy reach of their places of work such as Coventry, Rugby, Leamington Spa and Banbury. Yet despite its growth, Southam, notable for the broached and pinnacled landmark spire of St James's parish church (*opposite*), has not been allowed to outgrow itself. It still qualifies for the 'small town' tag when compared with its grander neighbours.

No amount of expansion, however, could detract from the town's long and chequered history, which Shakespeare alluded to in *Henry VI Part III*: 'At Southam I did leave him with his forces and do expect him here some two hours hence', says Sir John Somerville, speaking of Clarence to Warwick the Kingmaker.

Formerly an important stopping-place for stagecoaches, Southam still possesses some of its old coaching inns, as well as numerous other fascinating buildings recalling its past. One of these, a half-timbered shop on Market Hill, was the local manor house at the time of the Civil War, and Charles I is said to have stayed here shortly before the Battle of Edgehill.

According to tradition, Charles had special coins made at Southam's 14th-century Olde Mint (*inset*), so that his troops could be paid, but whether the story is true or not, it's certain that trade tokens were minted here, at least until the 18th century. Today, plastic credit cards are as likely to be seen as coins at the Olde Mint, as the building is a popular inn and restaurant.

The Stoneythorpe Hotel, once an infirmary for eye and ear disorders, has a fascinating link with medical history. It was in a cottage on the site of the hotel's forecourt that in 1823 Henry Lilley Smith founded the country's first provident dispensary – an early precursor of the National Health Service. His venture, recorded on a stone monument, may have something to do with the fact that in fields nearby is Southam's famous Holy Well, the ice-cold waters of which were supposed to cure eye ailments.

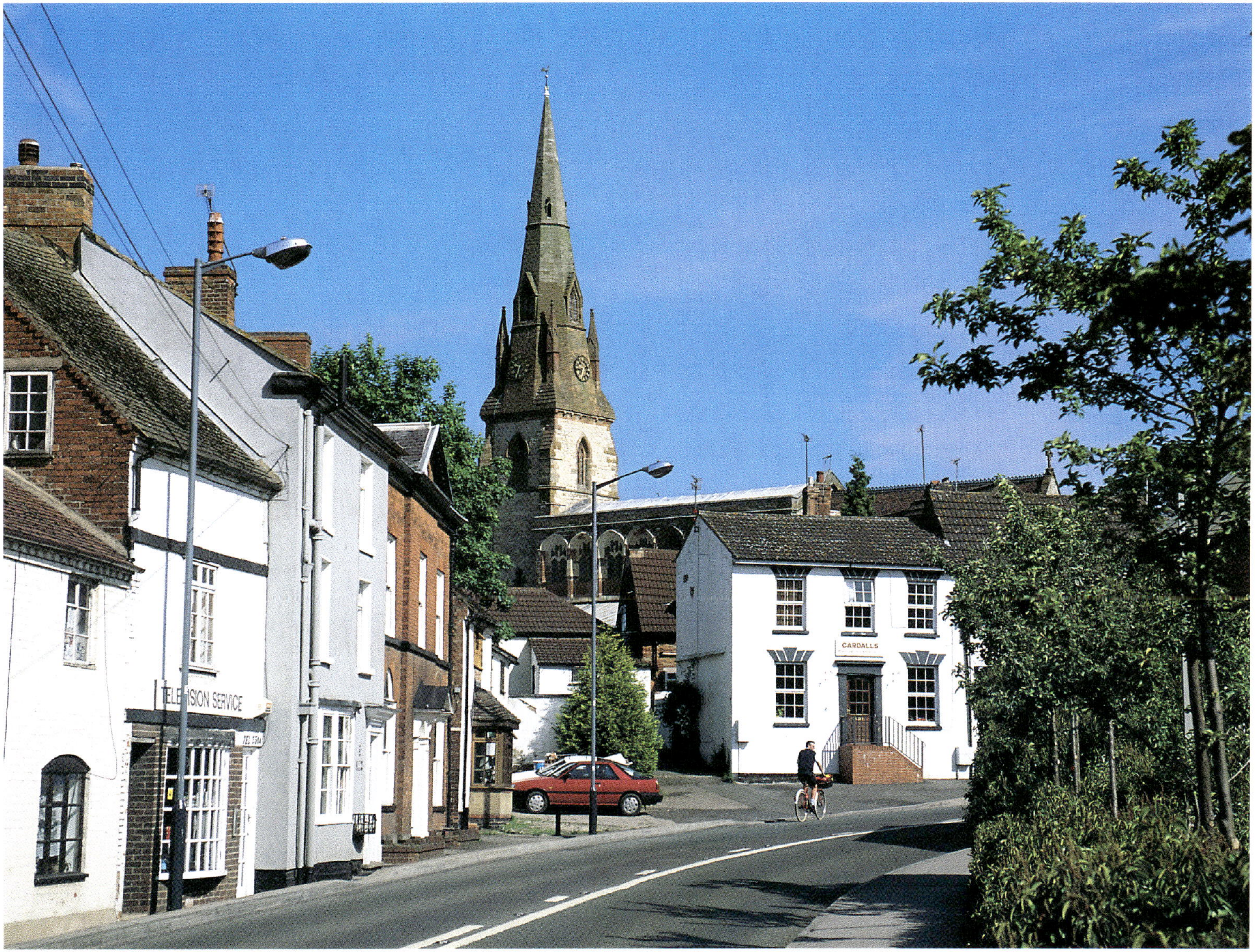
CARDALLS

Napton-on-the-Hill and Priors Hardwick

If there were a tautology prize for Warwickshire place-names, Napton-on-the-Hill, a few miles to the east of Southam, would probably win it. Napton is Anglo-Saxon for 'hilltop village', which makes the modern 'on-the-hill' suffix superfluous. It's rare, in any event, for a settlement to have developed on such a lofty, wind-blown prominence, as early builders usually favoured the more sheltered valleys lower down. Napton has thus earned itself a certain topographical distinction.

From their 500-foot-high vantage point on a clear day, the villagers are said to be able to see seven counties, a striking panorama which includes the picturesque Oxford Canal (*opposite*). This peaceful 18th-century waterway, which joins the Grand Union Canal at Napton, travels round the hill on three sides, a fact which delights the modern leisure-seekers as much as it tested the patience of the old bargees anxious to leave Napton behind and get on their way.

Napton itself is a pleasant village, recorded in the Domesday Book, and once boasting the status of a small and influential town with its own fair and market. Nowadays, its principal claims to fame include its historic Norman church of St Lawrence and its restored stone-built windmill, the white-painted sails of which are a familiar hilltop landmark for many miles around.

This is Warwickshire and Northamptonshire borderland country at its most rural, an area in which villages are relatively few and far between. Apart from Napton, two of the most notable are Priors Marston and Priors Hardwick, their ancient names recalling early links with the priors of the Benedictine monastery of Coventry.

History apart, Priors Hardwick has earned itself an indelible mark on the gastronomic map of the Midlands through its 16th-century village inn, the Butcher's Arms, which is now a restaurant of international repute. Ironically, its colourful garden (*inset*) attracts almost as much attention as its menus, and regularly delights visitors from far beyond Priors Hardwick's boundaries.

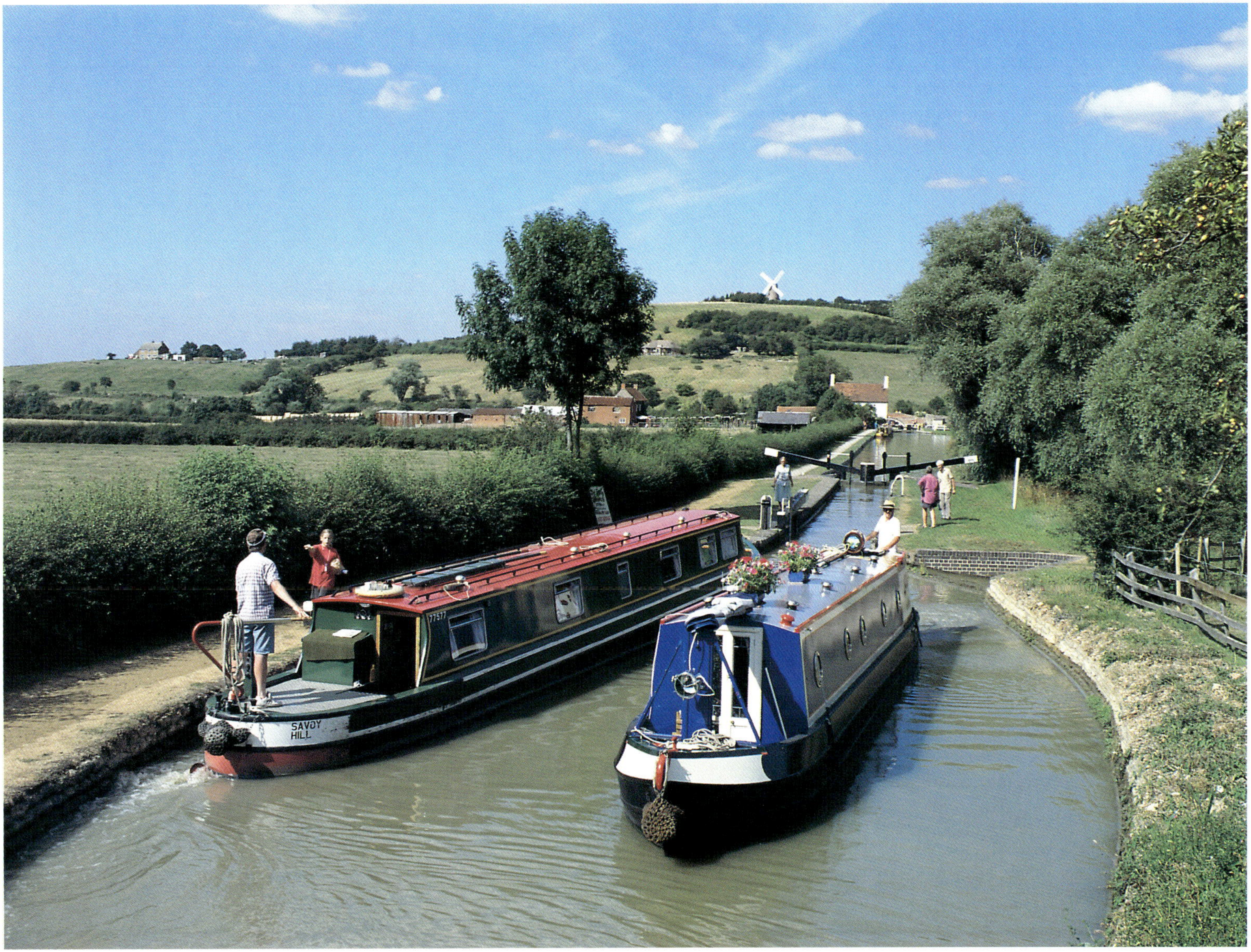
SAVOY
HILL

Draycote Water and Thurlaston

Some 600 acres of low-lying farmland between Dunchurch and the valley of the river Leam were flooded to become the much-needed reservoir known today as Draycote Water. It takes its name from the hamlet of Draycote on the very edge of the inundation, and as one of the region's largest man-made lakes, it allows Severn Trent Water to meet the growing domestic and industrial needs of a wide surrounding area. It has also become a major sporting and leisure attraction for yachtsmen and fishermen (*opposite*), as well as the focal point for the adjacent country park run by Warwickshire County Council.

Draycote Water is encircled by several villages, their names evocative of Warwickshire's rural history – Kites Hardwick and Leamington Hastings, Birdingbury and Frankton, Bourton-on-Dunsmore and Thurlaston. The last-named, sandwiched between Draycote Water's northern limits and the M45 motorway, is an off-the-beaten-track place in the literal sense. The only way in and out of it is over a narrow bridge spanning the motorway, a fact which leaves the village delightfully undisturbed in a little world of its own.

Although, with 20th-century inevitability, Thurlaston has had to meet the needs of the commuter age with new housing, it still retains much of its old character. There's even a sprinkling of thatch among the older cottages, while a former windmill which lost its sails around the time of the First World War has been converted into an attractive house. Another reminder of Thurlaston's past is the old village stocks (*inset*), in which local offenders once paid their debt to society. Nowadays, the stocks survive as a much-prized curiosity, their role in the pursuance of summary justice long forgotten.

Curious in a different context is the red-brick Victorian church of St Edmund, overlooking Draycote Water, more correctly described as a chapel of ease linked to the parish church at nearby Dunchurch. Its west tower is used as an unusual private residence, a reminder that the church was built originally as the village school, when the tower provided convenient accommodation for the schoolteacher.

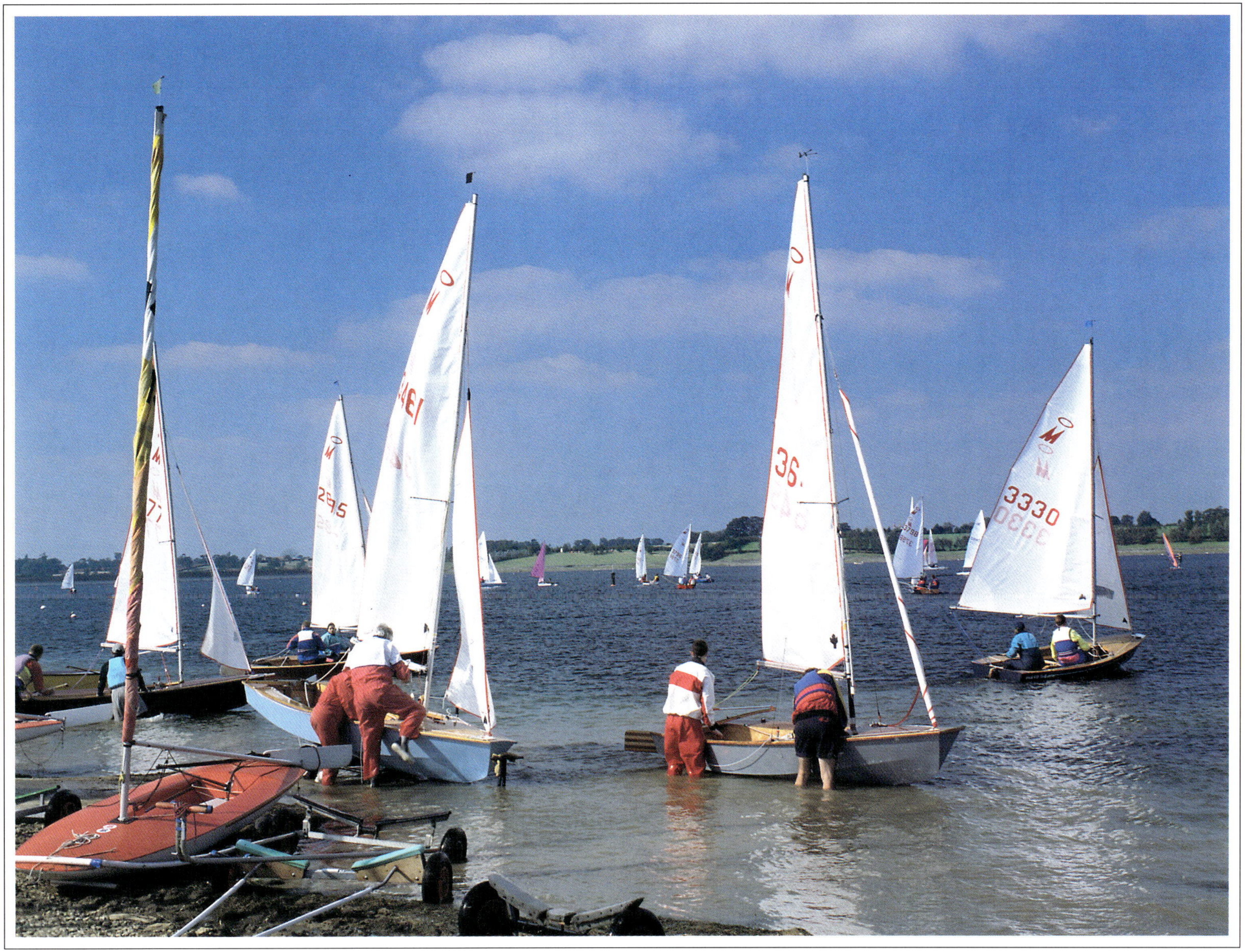
3330

Dunchurch

As Warwickshire villages go, Dunchurch is among the larger, and it has good reason to be grateful for the building of a motorway. Just to the south-west of Rugby, the village once straddled the A45 trunk road, which gave it more than its fair share of through traffic. It is still a busy place, but much of the heavy traffic which once thronged the village on its way between Coventry and the east, now bypasses it along the M45 motorway. As a result, the wealth of old buildings which give Dunchurch so much of its character (*opposite*) breathe an almost audible sigh of relief.

Ironically, it was the trade generated by passing traffic which, to a large extent, moulded the village's destiny long before the internal combustion engine was invented.

Dunchurch was an important staging post on two busy cross-country stagecoach routes, and the numerous coaching inns found themselves doing brisk business. Several of these fine old hostelries continue to thrive, contributing to the village's popularity with its modern-day visitors.

Dunchurch can, in fact, claim a long and eventful history, and it was already a community of some importance at the time of the Domesday Book in 1086 when it was owned by a Norman nobleman. It became a busy market town, more important than neighbouring Rugby, but the railway mania of the Victorians led to Rugby's subsequent development, leaving Dunchurch to its own devices. One of the village's more cherished historical claims is that the thatched house once occupied by the local smithy and still known as the Old Forge, complete with its spreading chestnut tree, was the inspiration for Longfellow when he wrote his celebrated poem *The Village Blacksmith*.

Gunpowder, treason and plot have also played a significant role in the history of Dunchurch. The former Old Lion Inn was the place where the conspirators spent the night while they awaited news of Guy Fawkes's attempt to blow up Parliament. In the event, all they received was news of his failure, but had the outcome been different, the whole course of English history could have changed, and Dunchurch's involvement would have been seen in quite a different light. As it is, the black-and-white timbered Old Lion Inn survives today as Guy Fawkes House (*inset*), its name plaque confirming its role in one of the more unsavoury episodes of English politics.

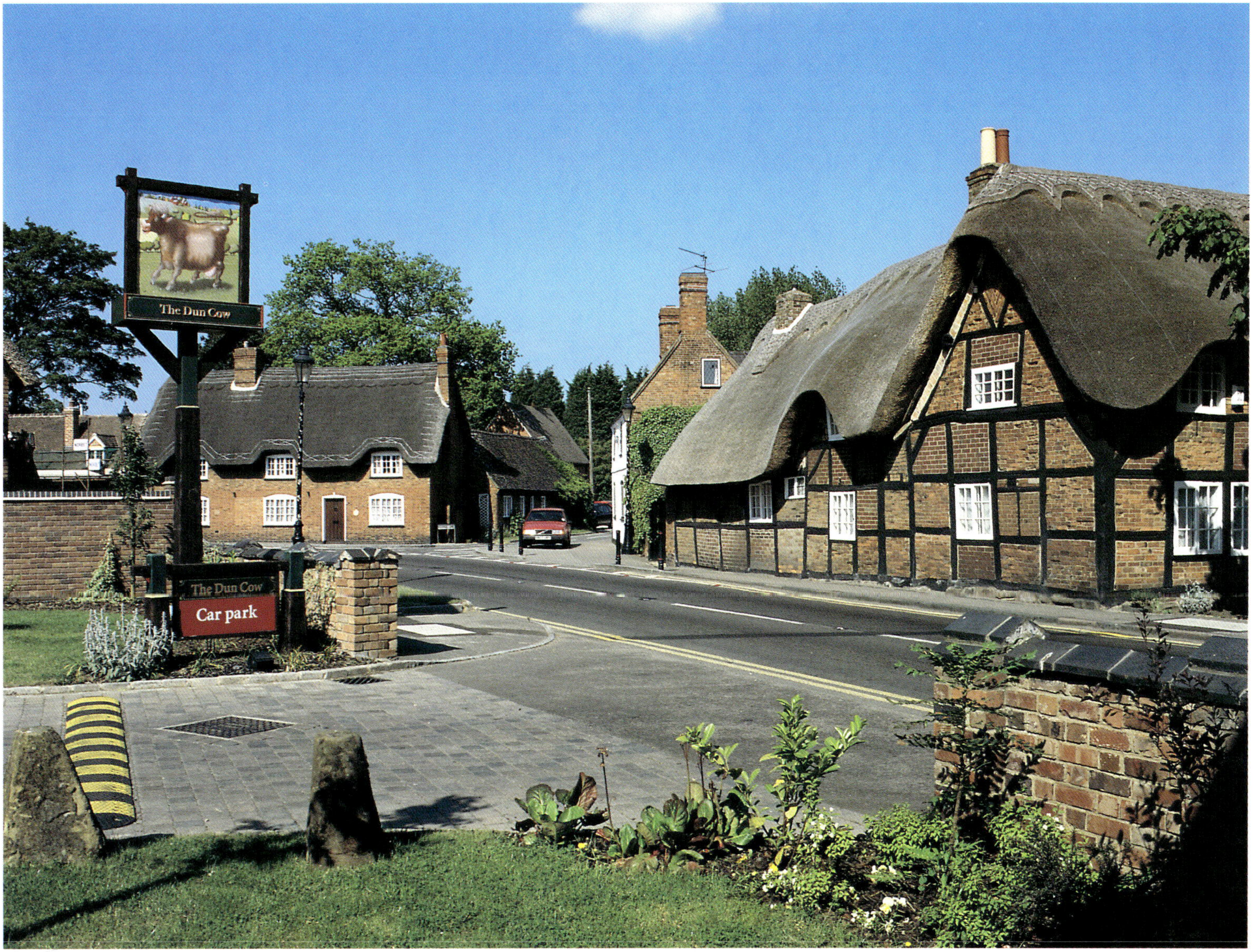
The Dun Cow
The Dun Cow
Car park

Rugby

The reputation of Rugby rests mainly on two aspects of its history – the founding of its famous public school and the advent of the railway.

When the London and Birmingham Railway reached Rugby in the 19th century, the Victorians, with their customary zeal, saw the opportunity not only to give the town a key role in their burgeoning railway network, but to develop it as an important centre of industry. Had they not done so, Rugby today would probably be no more than a modest-sized market town, but with the distinction that it possessed a famous public school. In the event, Rugby is now counted among the region's largest and most important industrial towns, and as a popular shopping centre (*inset*) serving a wide surrounding area.

When Lawrence Sheriff, a 16th-century London grocer, made provision in his will for the education of boys in Rugby, he would not even have dreamed that the school which his money founded would evolve into one of the best-known educational establishments in the world. Today, Rugby and its school are inseparable. The great complex of historic school buildings and playing fields (*opposite*) dominates the town centre as succeeding generations of boys (and now girls) follow in the footsteps of their many illustrious predecessors.

The roll of Old Rugbeians reads like a *Who's Who* of household names, including such distinguished former pupils as the poet Rupert Brooke; William Temple, Archbishop of Canterbury; Charles Lutwidge Dodgson who, as Lewis Carroll, wrote *Alice's Adventures in Wonderland*; Thomas Arnold, who became one of the school's most influential headmasters; and of course Judge Thomas Hughes who immortalised school life at Rugby in *Tom Brown's Schooldays*.

In 1878, another well-known school was opened in the town, bearing the name of Rugby School's founder, Lawrence Sheriff. Unlike its older neighbour, Lawrence Sheriff School was established specifically to cater for local boys rather than for those from a much wider area and even from overseas.

One former pupil of Rugby School whose name has gone down in the annals of sporting history is William Webb Ellis. In 1823, according to a school plaque, he demonstrated 'a fine disregard for the rules of football as played in his time', by picking up the ball in his arms and running with it. He was thus the unwitting originator of the sport, now played throughout the world, to which the school has given its name.

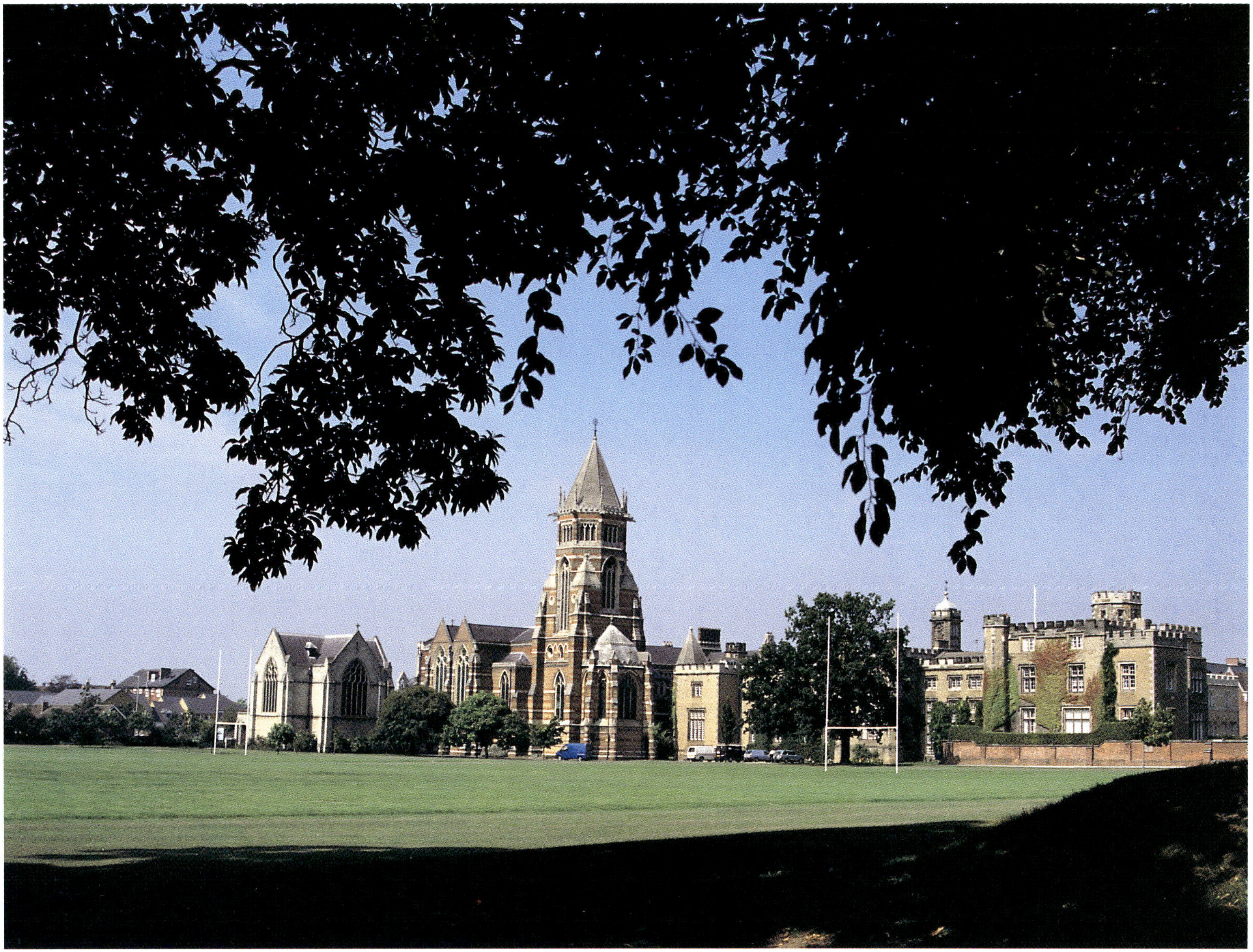

Wolston and King's Newnham

Wolston, almost midway between Coventry and Rugby, may not figure among Warwickshire's most renowned villages, although the little stream and the old cottages bordering the main street (*opposite*), have attracted more than a few artists and photographers over the years.

For a place with such a long and fascinating history it deserves to be better known than it is. It can even claim to have played a brief but significant role in England's troubled religious history, thanks to the clandestine activities of the Welsh non-conformist John Penry in the 16th century. Penry set up one of his illegal printing presses in Wolston's Benedictine priory to produce his inflammatory Martin Marprelate tracts aimed against the established church. The old priory has long since disappeared, although parts of it are incorporated in the attractive Elizabethan house which stands on the site today.

The parish church of St Margaret can also claim a long and eventful history. Although little if anything of its Saxon origins remain, the Normans have left their mark in no uncertain manner, as have the builders of succeeding centuries, with the result that the church is a splendid amalgam of architectural styles.

Close to the church a narrow bridge over the Avon links Wolston to its near neighbour Brandon, a village which until the 13th century boasted its own castle. Today, only scant remains of this once mighty fortification still exist on the river bank opposite Wolston church, but like the prehistoric round barrow on nearby Lammas Hill, it is an interesting site for the local historians.

A few miles to the north-east, another more poignant reminder of the past is the surviving tower of King's Newnham church (*inset*), strangely isolated in its farmland setting, where grazing sheep have long since replaced the erstwhile parishioners. Nowadays, King's Newnham consists of no more than a handful of buildings, although Georgian Newnham Hall still stands proudly by the old church tower.

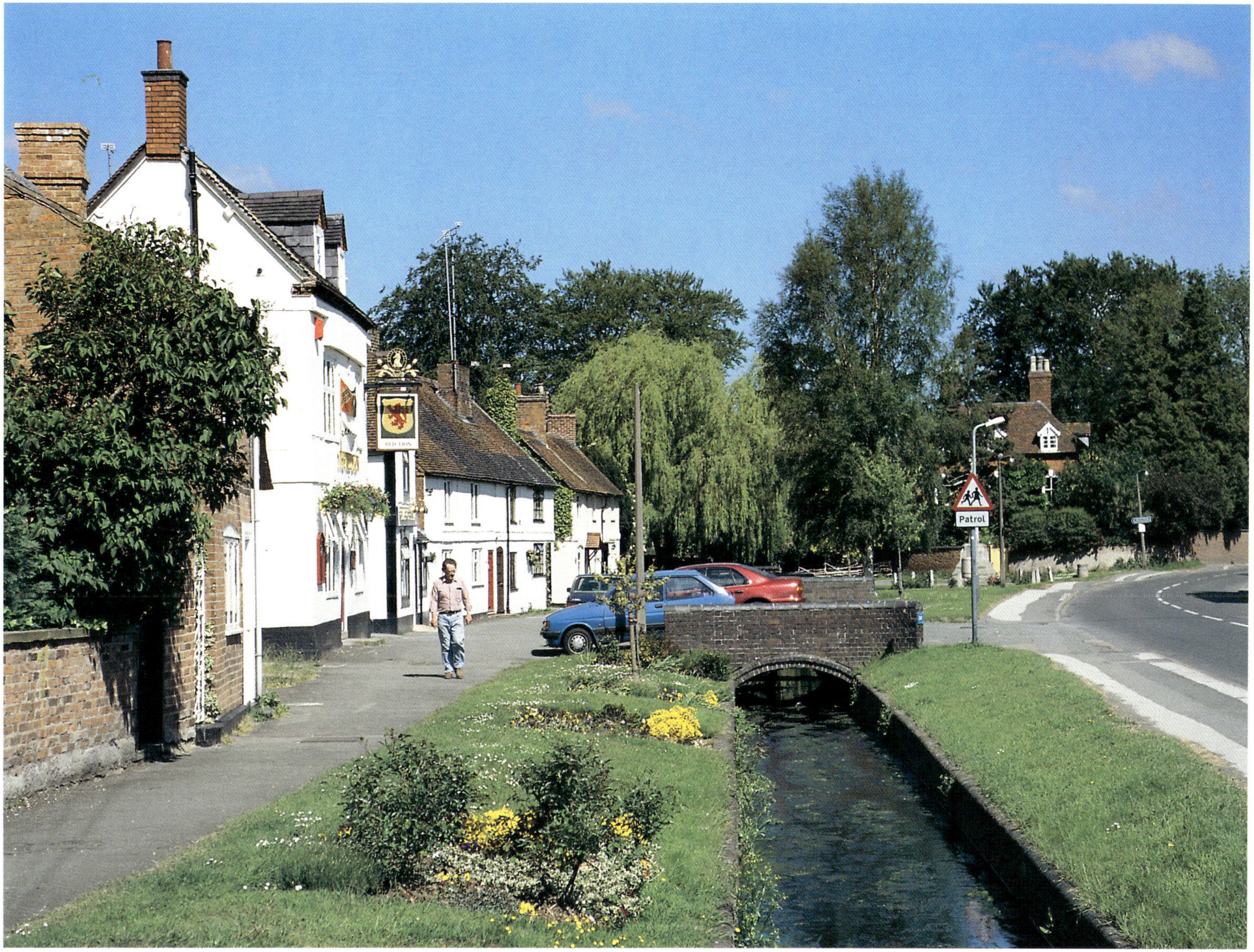
Patrol

Coombe Abbey and Brinklow

Lancelot 'Capability' Brown would still be able to recognise much of his 18th-century landscaping of Coombe Abbey's parkland – especially the vast ornamental lake – which he carried out for William, sixth Baron Craven, even though the grounds are now a popular country park. The focal point of the park is the great mansion of Coombe Abbey itself (*opposite*), a house with a long and fascinating history stretching back over many centuries. Originally a Cistercian monastery founded in 1150, it was largely demolished, not surprisingly, during the reign of Henry VIII, although the building that replaced it incorporated several monastic features which can still be seen today.

For generations the home of the Craven family, Coombe Abbey was again the subject of considerable rebuilding in the 19th century before the entire estate was sold in the 1920s, much of it to a Coventry builder. The house later became a rather splendid hall of residence for GEC apprentices until it was purchased, with much of the land, by its present owners, Coventry City Council. The Council, with commendable foresight, designated the magnificent grounds as a country park, and leased the house to a hotel company which has ensured it a place among the leading visitor attractions of the Midlands through the popular medieval banquets which are regularly held here.

Although Coventry suburbia now virtually rubs shoulders with the western side of Coombe Country Park, there is still plenty of unspoilt countryside to the east towards the neighbouring village of Brinklow, which, like Coombe Abbey, is a place steeped in history. It is built on a hill, possibly the site of an early burial mound, around which the Romans took the unusual step of diverting their normally unwavering Fosse Way. In the reign of King Stephen, the Mowbray family constructed a motte-and-bailey castle here, the remains of which are among the best surviving examples in Britain.

The parish church (*inset*) contains many interesting features including remnants of an earlier building belonging to the Austin Canons of Kenilworth. In the churchyard, one of the tombstones is a poignant reminder of a local deaf and dumb woodcutter, bearing representations of his trade: a bundle of faggots, a glove, an axe and a woodcutter's hook.

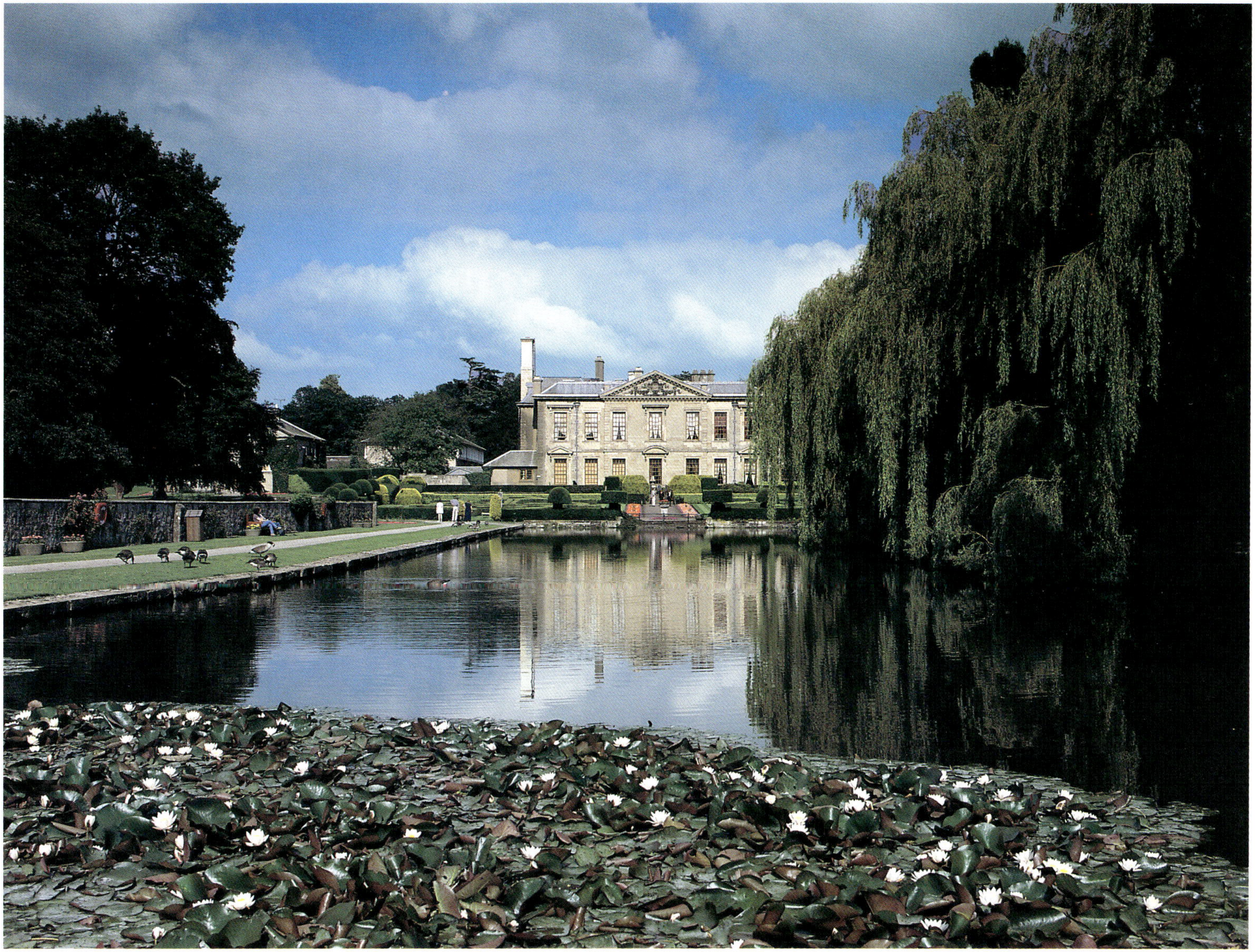

Coventry

The fateful night of 14th November 1940 changed the face of Coventry for ever. Hitler's bombs wiped out much of the city centre, reducing the old Cathedral of St Michael to a charred ruin and demolishing shops, factories, offices and houses. The scale of devastation was so enormous that it gave a new word to the English language – the verb 'to coventrate', meaning to suffer virtual obliteration.

The city's subsequent recovery has been well documented and is symbolised by Sir Basil Spence's bold new cathedral adjoining the surviving ruins of the old (*opposite*). Around it a brave new city centre sprang up, planned on the grand scale and encircled by a largely elevated ring-road. The modern Coventry we see today bears little resemblance to the pre-war city, although miraculously more than a few important historic buildings did survive the bombing to provide evocative links with the past. In ancient Spon Street, a number of valuable timbered buildings have been re-erected from other parts of the city to re-create a 'living' medieval thoroughfare.

Coventry's proud industrial heritage lives on unscathed, its roots embedded in the medieval trade guilds and the once-flourishing wool industry on which the city's early prosperity was founded. Later came the silk weavers and the ribbon- and watch-makers, and in more recent years the bicycle and car manufacturers whose products have boosted Coventry's unique industrial reputation throughout the world.

No less well known than Coventry's industrial prowess is the endearing story of Lady Godiva, whose name is inseparable from that of the city itself. Whether or not she did ride naked round the streets in the 11th century, in order to persuade her husband, Earl Leofric, to 'deliver the city from a burdensome and most shameful bondage' is open to question, but the legend lives on. Today, the impressive statue of Godiva on horseback which graces the redeveloped Broadgate (*inset*), endures as a bold focal point in the city centre.

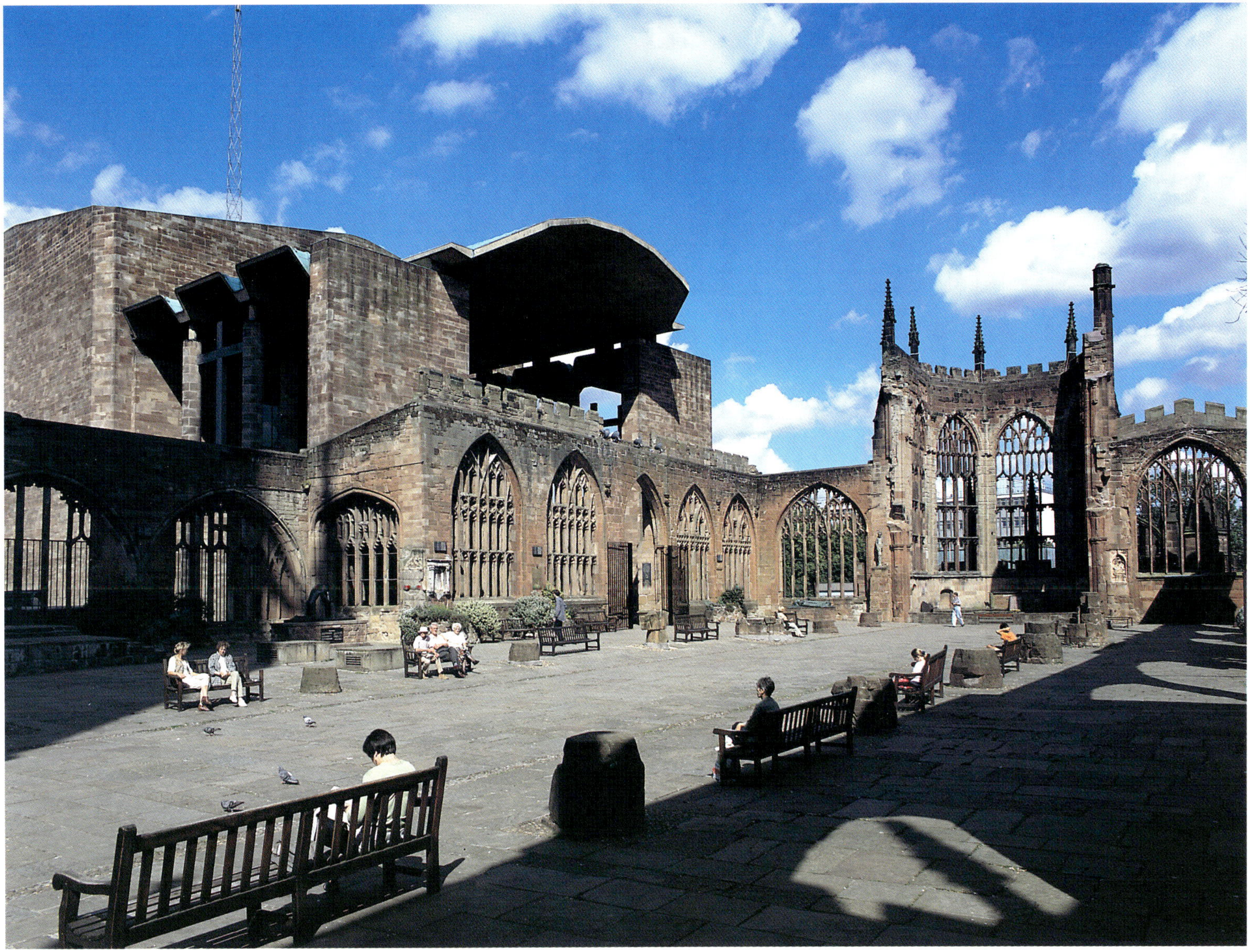

Berkswell

Given its geographical position between the sprawling conurbations of Birmingham and Coventry, the village of Berkswell (*inset*) can count itself fortunate that it continues to survive as a place of considerable rural charm and character.

The historian Sir Nikolaus Pevsner describes Berkswell church as 'easily the most interesting village church in Warwickshire', and he was never a writer to indulge in hyperbole. It is certainly a rare architectural treasure, distinguished by its unusual two-storey timbered porch resembling a diminutive cottage. An amusing exercise for observant visitors is to try to spot the church mice. These are the carved trademarks of the woodcarver Robert Thompson, whose craftsmanship includes the fine oak font and various other carvings in the church. His mice can also be spotted in Ilmington church in the south of the county, mentioned on page 10.

By the side of the church stands the 17th-century former rectory known as Well House, its name alluding to the nearby stone-lined pond on the site of the original baptismal well from which the village derives its name. Well House is just one of several notable buildings in and around the village, such as 19th-century Berkswell Hall, Ram Hall built in about 1600, half-timbered Nailcote Hall, now a popular hotel and country club (*opposite*), and a delightful row of Victorian red-brick almshouses.

A Berkswell curiosity is the old village stocks which have five holes. The story goes that they originally had just four to accommodate two local wrongdoers, but the fifth was added when a third offender proved to be a man with one leg. Another curiosity is the fearsome looking cannon at the 16th-century Bear Inn. It's a relic from the Crimean War, and a charming incongruity in so peaceful a setting. Berkswell can even boast its own museum in an attractive timbered cottage by the village almshouses. Appropriately, the theme of its collection is local rural life, and it contains some fascinating bygones.

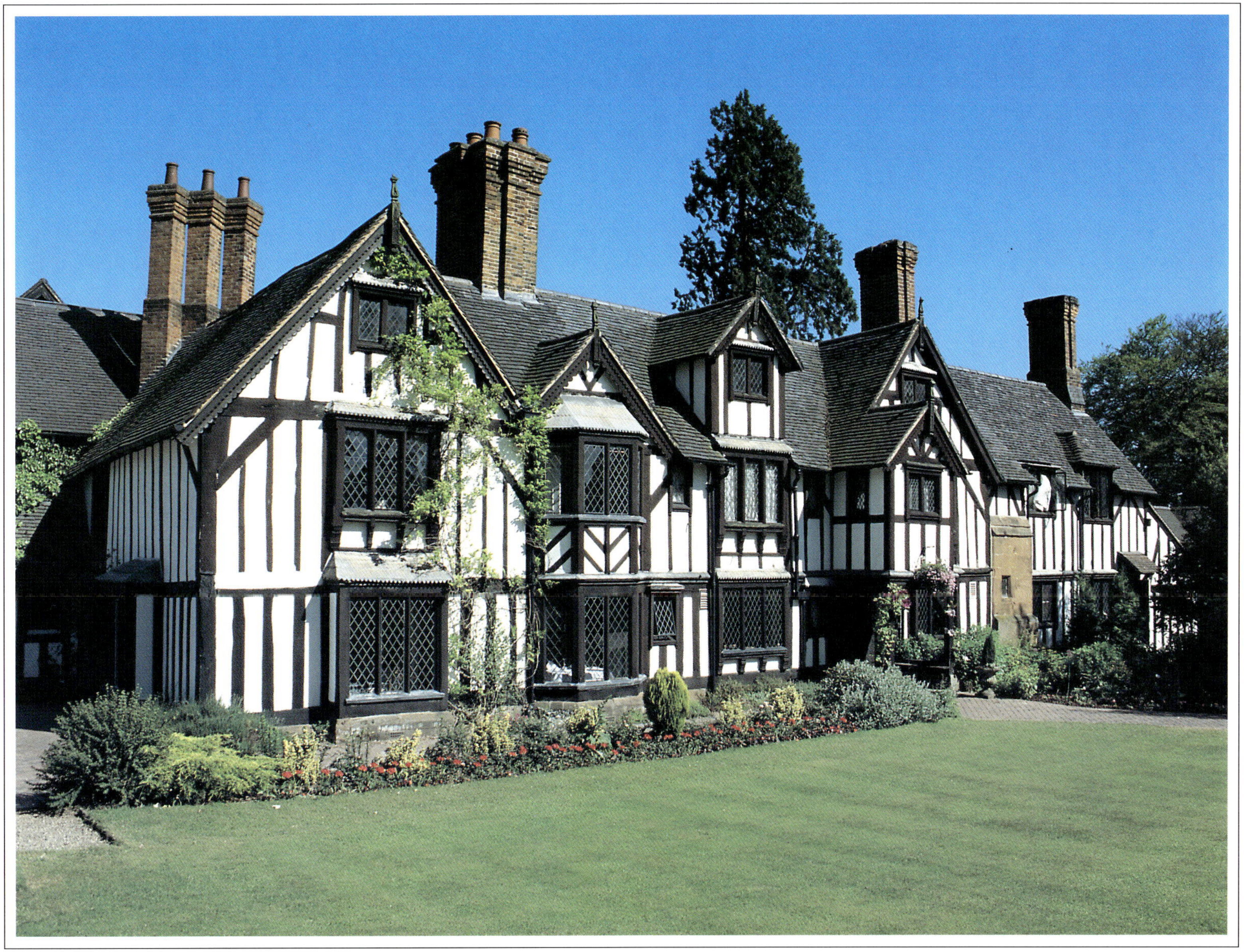

Meriden

Although Lillington near Leamington Spa may fiercely contest the claim, Meriden stakes its reputation on being at the exact centre of England. The village conveniently ignores the fact that Lillington's Midland Oak (or to be more precise, one of the original tree's progeny) is also said to mark this revered geographical spot.

There are other contenders to the claim, too, but Meriden is arguably the favourite, and its 500-year-old Centre of England cross on the green (*opposite*) is proudly quoted when any lingering doubts are voiced. Just to make sure, a Centre of England oak tree was planted in the village in 1962. It also marked the opening of the bypass which, in the nick of time, relieved Meriden of imminent strangulation by the incessant traffic travelling between Birmingham and Coventry. A plaque by the tree proclaims that when the bypass was built, 'Meriden became a village once again', a role it has zealously guarded during the ensuing years, despite the many new housing developments which have taken place.

Meriden's parish church of St Lawrence, its Norman origins still much in evidence, stands symbolically on a hilltop away from the village centre, a reminder that this lofty site was where the community originally grew up. But the hill proved an obstacle for passing travellers seeking sustenance in coaching days, and the village's development continued on the main road down below, where hostelries were more accessible.

The picturesque village pond (*inset*) is another of Meriden's attractions, along with some notable historic houses which still survive. Among these are the timber-framed medieval Moat House, the early 18th-century Meriden Hall, and the much enlarged Manor House now transformed into a hotel. Forest Hall, another notable survivor, was built by Joseph Bonomi in 1788 for the Woodmen of Arden, the oldest archery club in the country, and it remains their headquarters to this day.

Meriden has a special place of affection in the hearts of the nation's cyclists, many of whom pedal here each May to congregate by the obelisk on the green which commemorates those of their number who fell in both world wars. Nearby, a stone seat bears this inscription: 'To the memory of Wayfarer (W. M. Robinson) 17 September 1956. His devotion to the pastime of cycling inspired many to enjoy the countryside and the open road. Erected on behalf of all cyclists by the Cyclists' Touring Club.'

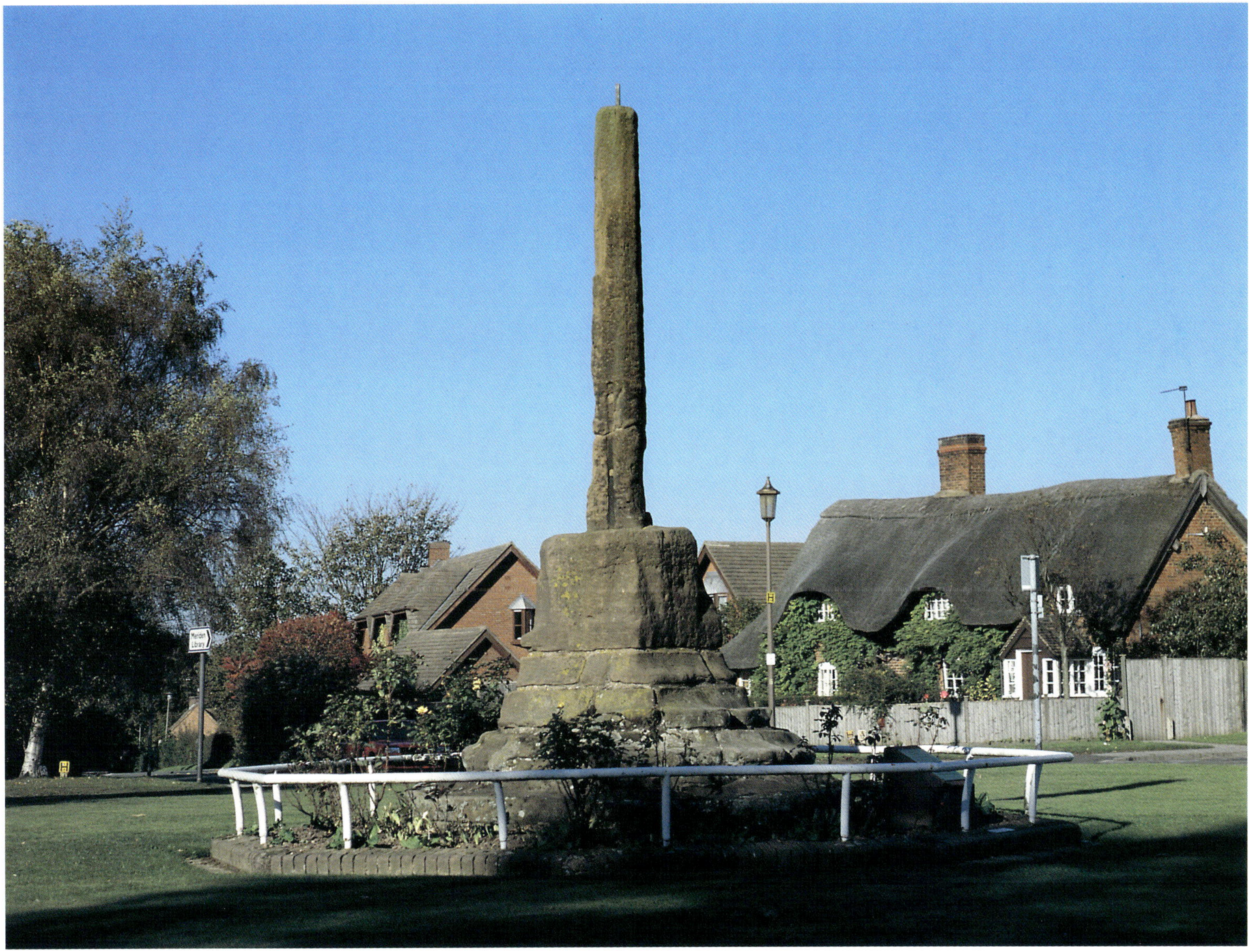

Packwood House

Warwickshire is well endowed with stately homes, several owned by the National Trust and open to the public. One such is delightful Packwood House near Hockley Heath (*opposite*), a timber-framed, multi-gabled mansion built in the 16th century for the Fetherston family. Although the original timbering is now hidden behind rendering, this has enhanced rather than detracted from Packwood's overall architectural entity. The interior recalls many notable episodes in the mansion's long history: the Ireton room is named after Cromwell's general, Henry Ireton, who spent the night here before the Battle of Edgehill in 1642, and Queen Mary's room recalls a royal visit of 1927. The Great Hall was formerly a detached barn offering shelter to cattle before it was linked to the main house in the 20th century.

Packwood was given to the National Trust in 1941 by the then owner Graham Baron Ash, whose own influence on the interior largely reflects the period between the two world wars. But earlier treasures remain, including a rare collection of 16th-century textiles and furniture.

For all its interior interest, Packwood is no less noted for its fine grounds, which include a magnificent Carolean garden bounded by four gazebos, and the famous garden of clipped yews planted originally by John Fetherston in the 17th century. This masterpiece of topiary is said to represent the Sermon on the Mount, with Christ as the most prominent yew of them all.

Just to the south of Packwood House, meandering its way through the Warwickshire countryside, is the Stratford-upon-Avon Canal, a picturesque 25-mile waterway which links the Avon at Stratford with the Worcester and Birmingham Canal at King's Norton. Its southern section, below the junction with the Grand Union Canal at Kingswood near Lapworth, was saved from dereliction in the 1960s by the efforts of volunteer workers, and was administered by the National Trust until taken over by British Waterways.

Today a popular haunt for holidaymakers, the canal retains much of its original character including its unique bridges and locks, and its quaint, barrel-roofed cottages (*inset*) built by the original navigation workers, or 'navvies'. As the roofing skills of these men were limited to canal tunnels, they employed a similar technique in building their cottages.

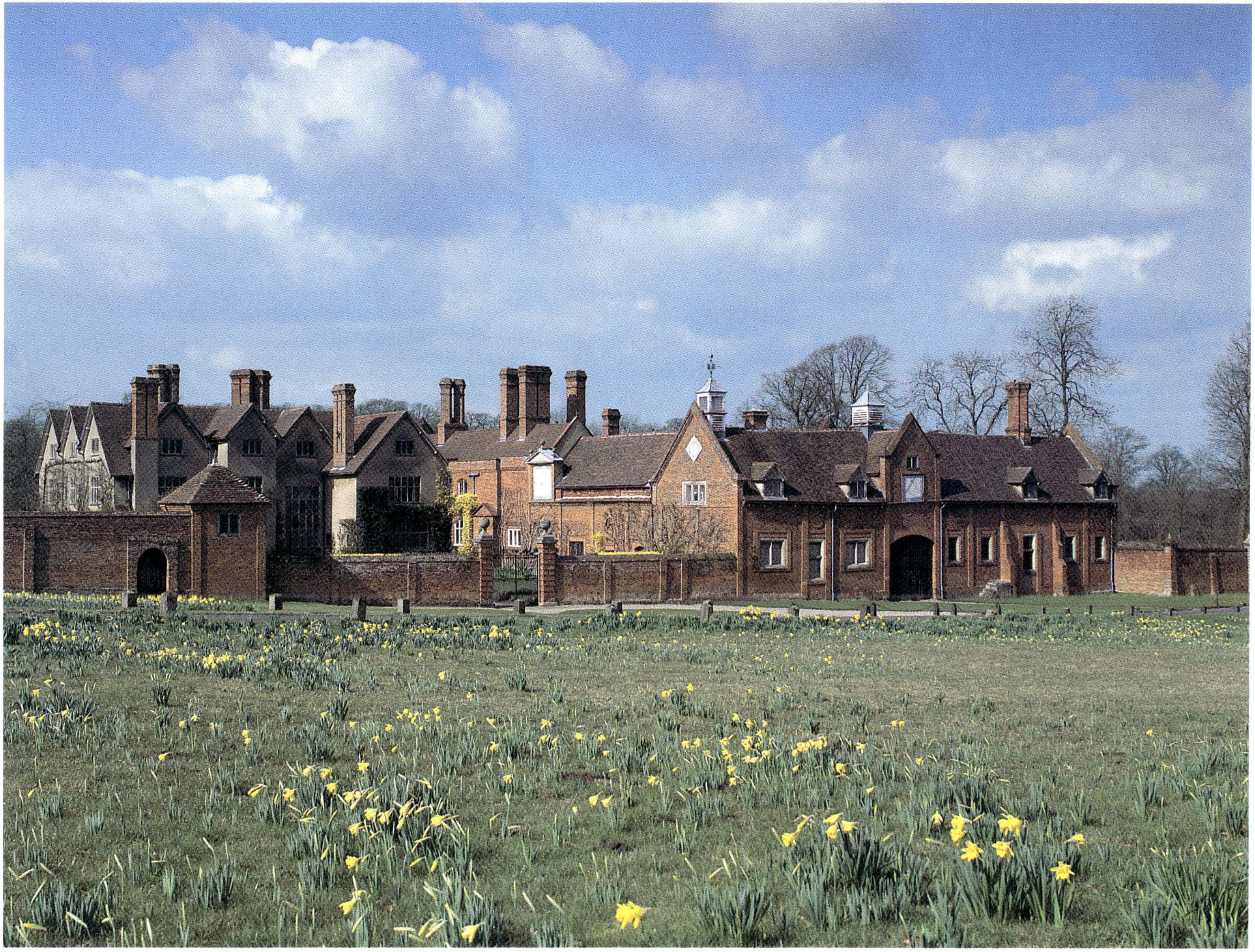

Earlswood Lakes

The scattered village of Earlswood is less than half a dozen miles from the southern edge of the Birmingham conurbation, a fact which its peaceful farmland setting makes it difficult to appreciate.

As a community, Earlswood has been on the map for many centuries, but it was not until the end of the 18th century that any appreciable growth took place. This was due almost entirely to the building of the nearby Stratford-upon-Avon Canal and the choice of Earlswood as the site of three giant reservoirs needed to keep the canal topped up with water. Today, the reservoirs are better known as Earlswood Lakes (*opposite*) and they have become an established feature of the landscape.

Although Earlswood Lakes are still enjoyed by anglers and sailing enthusiasts, their popularity today is hardly comparable with that of the early years of the 20th century. In those days, charabancs would bring crowds of day trippers here for a few hours of lakeside enjoyment. With an eye on a lucrative business opportunity, the locals provided refreshments for the visitors and even charged twopence for the safe custody of bicycles.

A curious reminder of the construction of the Stratford Canal exists in the nearby village of Tanworth-in-Arden. The men who built the canal were evidently not particularly law-abiding, a fact which prompted the villagers to found the Tanworth Association for the Prosecution of Felons. Today, even though lawless navvies no longer pose a threat, the association still exists, but primarily as a social institution.

Tanworth itself (*inset*) is a delightfully self-contained village which has managed to preserve much of its traditional character. A notable landmark for many miles around is the distinctive broach spire of the 14th-century parish church of St Mary Magdalene, while a track across the fields leads to noble Umberslade Hall, now converted into luxury apartments. The mansion was formerly the family seat of the Archers, rebuilt in the 17th century for Andrew Archer, brother of the architect Thomas Archer who designed Birmingham Cathedral. The tall obelisk in the grounds is said to commemorate the elevation to the peerage of Andrew Archer's son, another Thomas, in 1747.

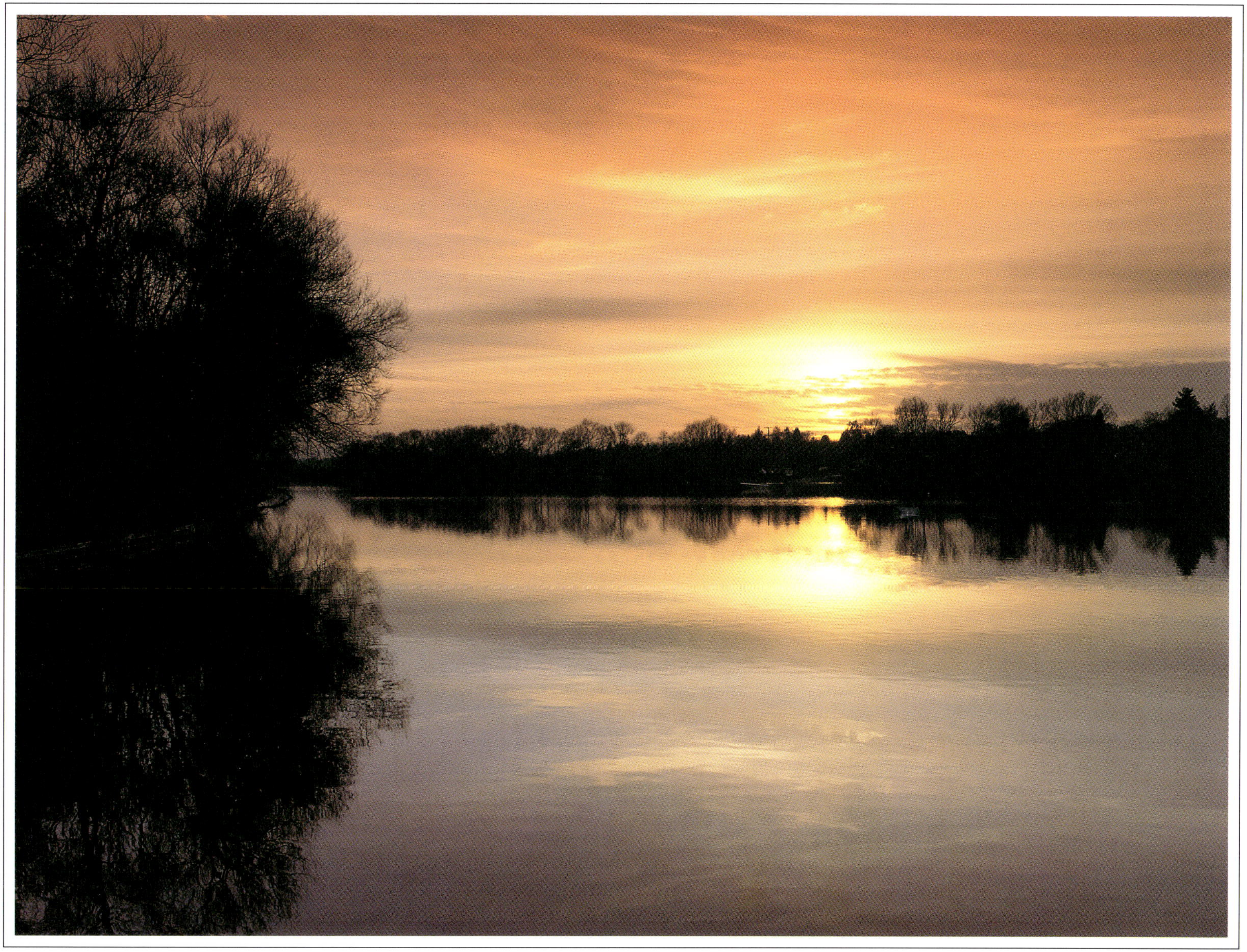

Knowle

Straddling the Warwick to Birmingham road just to the south of Solihull, the village of Knowle possesses a certain distinctive individuality which local inhabitants nurture. Even the term 'village' is jealously guarded, although nowadays, in the strictly rural sense, it's something of an affectionate anachronism.

Knowle has a long history, and several of its older timber-framed buildings still exist as reminders of the days when it really was a village, long before its inevitable expansion in the 20th century. Among these architectural gems is 15th-century Chester House in the busy High Street (*opposite*), now serving as a delightfully unusual public library. One writer has suggested, rather pointedly, that the centre of Knowle is characterised by 'Stockbroker's Tudor and Banker's Georgian'. It may be a slightly misleading generalisation, but it's an interesting comment which says as much about the village's perceived social status as it does about its architecture.

No less than three saints are the dedicatees of Knowle's parish church – John the Baptist, Lawrence and Anne – a fittingly prestigious arrangement for so stately a place of worship which can trace its roots back to a 14th-century chapel. In the shadow of the church's lofty battlemented tower stands the 15th-century timber-framed Guild House, another architectural treasure of which Knowle can be justly proud.

A short distance to the east of Knowle, on the winding road to Balsall Common, lies the hamlet of Temple Balsall, its name revealing historical links with the Knights Templar, the military religious order founded in the 12th century to protect pilgrims to the Holy Land. The Templars had a preceptory here, and their chapel now serves as the parish church, one of the best examples of its date in the Midlands.

History is everywhere in Temple Balsall, and it is remarkable that in a place as small as this, so many buildings have a story to tell. The Lady Katherine Leveson Hospital, founded in 1677 by a granddaughter of Robert Dudley, Earl of Leicester, is an eloquent example. Its pedimented red-brick almshouses (*inset*) face each other across a grassy courtyard, watched over by the Master's House of 1836 with its twin Tudor-style towers, one bearing a clock and the other a sundial.

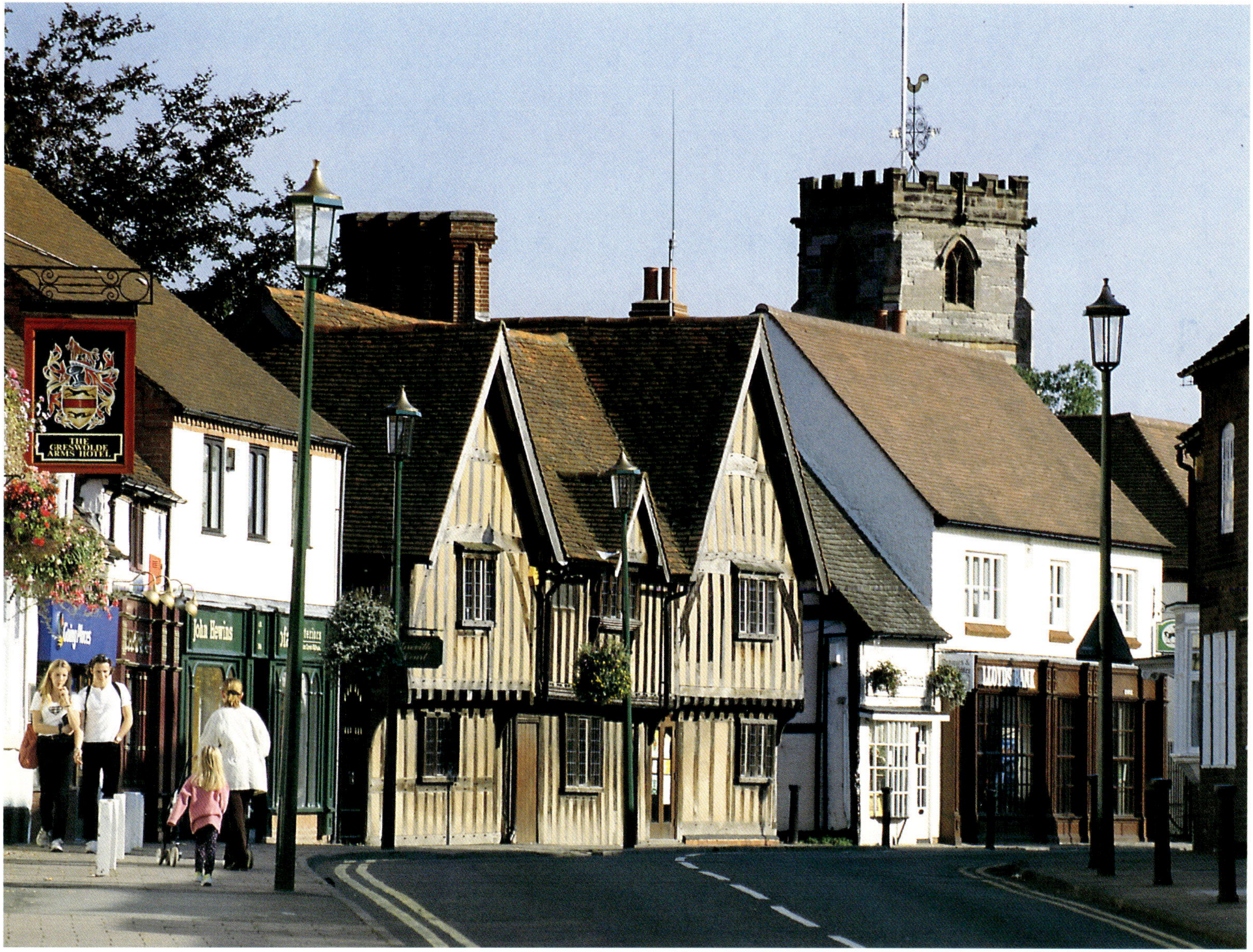
THE GRESWOLDE ARMS HOTEL
John Hewins
LLOYDS BANK

Solihull

The motto of Solihull Metropolitan Borough Council is *Urbs in Rure* – the town in the country – and it's a claim which, despite the inevitable pressures of building development in recent years, still holds more than a grain of truth. Open countryside, if not exactly surrounding Solihull, certainly comprises much of its borderland.

Although the town is an ancient place (once little more than a forest settlement, it gained its own market as early as 1242), it has developed over the centuries into one of the busiest commercial and industrial towns of the Midlands, and is now among the region's most popular residential areas. At the hub is Mell Square, a spacious shopping precinct distinguished by its 1980s sculpture of a mother, father and child by John Ravera entitled, aptly for its location, 'Family Outing' (*inset*).

The hallmark of many successful modern towns these days would seem to be a pedestrianised High Street, and Solihull is no exception. But even in this busy, car-free thoroughfare the past is not entirely forgotten. Among the modern shops, with a delightful touch of incongruity, stands the old manor house. Built by the influential Greswold family in 1495, it serves the community today as a much-used local meeting-place. Close by, another reminder of the older Solihull exists more or less intact. This is The Square (*opposite*), dominated by the largely 13th-century parish church dedicated to St Alphege, an 11th-century Archbishop of Canterbury, and topped by the slender spire which is the town's most familiar landmark.

Solihull has many assets in which it can justly take pride, ranging from the famous school of ancient foundation which shares the town's name, to the birthplace of the ubiquitous Land Rover. Further feathers in its cap are the National Exhibition Centre and Birmingham International Airport. Contrary to popular belief, neither of these famous sites is in Birmingham; both, as it happens, are within the boundaries of the Metropolitan Borough of Solihull.

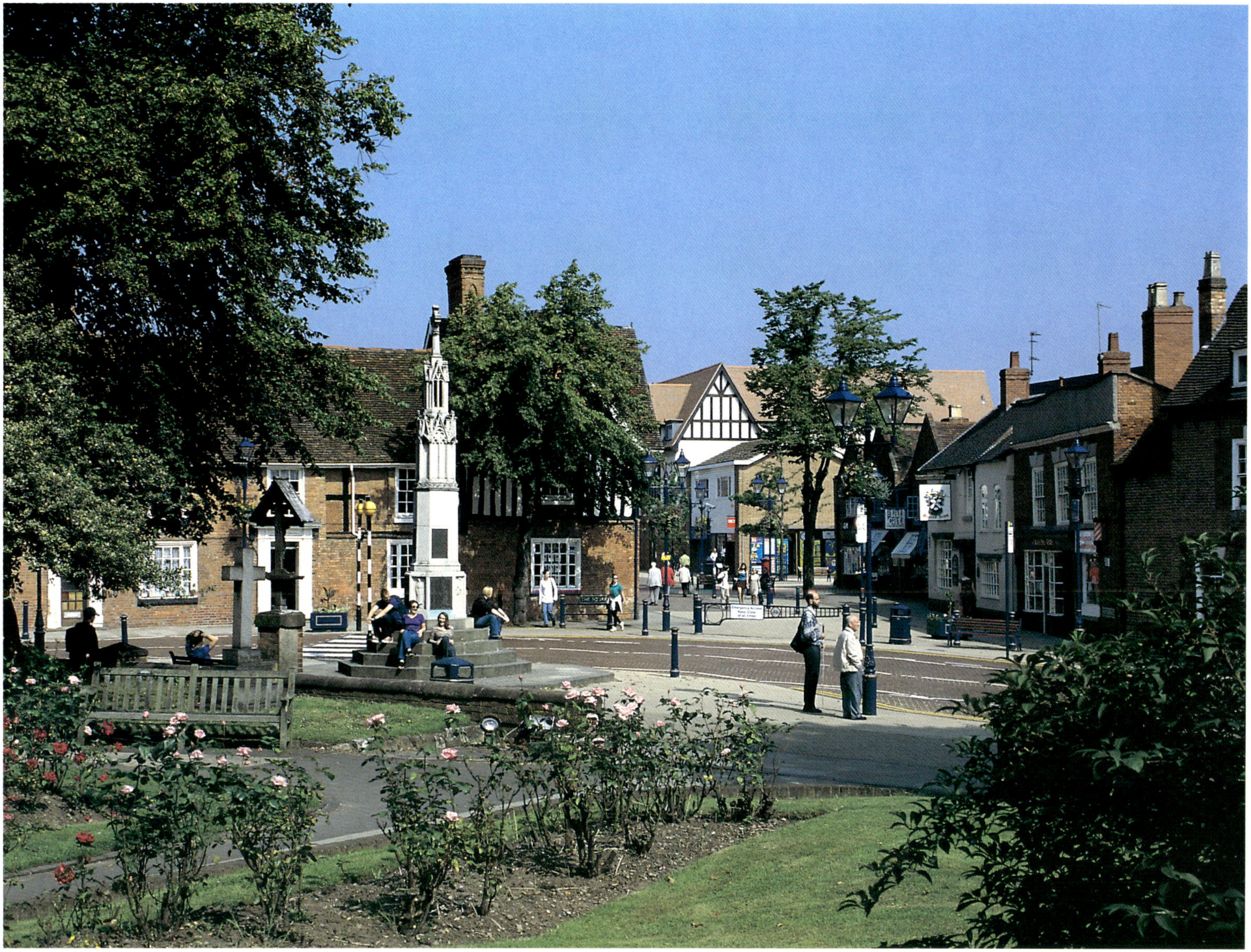

Coleshill

In the heyday of the stagecoach, when the old market town of Coleshill was a good deal smaller than it is today, its position on the main route between London and the north-west gave it considerable importance. This was where horses were changed and mail was offloaded for Birmingham, and there were more than 20 inns in the town to cope with all the comings and goings.

Until the Second World War, Coleshill's long main street, which climbs over a prominent town-centre hill before descending to cross the river Cole over a fine 16th-century stone-arched bridge, was part of the busy road from Coventry to Lichfield. A timely bypass may have eased the threat of congestion for a while, but the town today, again has more than enough traffic to cope with.

Coleshill is, in fact, a place of great antiquity, having flourished as an established settlement in Saxon times, and later being proclaimed a royal manor by the Normans. Today, among its many modern buildings, there are still some notable examples of half-timbered, Georgian and Victorian architecture to add a touch of distinction to the town centre, and the pleasing variety of styles and differing roof-lines in the main street is one of Coleshill's visual attractions.

But the town's most notable building is its medieval parish church of St Peter and St Paul, elaborately restored by the Victorians and containing one of the finest carved Norman fonts in the country. The slender steeple, rising to a height of some 170 feet, is a much-loved local landmark seen at its most impressive over the quiet watermeadows of the Cole to the north of the town (*opposite*). Close to the church, on Church Hill, stand the old town stocks, an evocative reminder of the days when local miscreants received summary justice for their misdeeds. This treasured relic is unique in Warwickshire, as it combines a whipping post and pillory.

Coleshill can also claim, on its eastern doorstep, one of the great castles of the Midlands, Maxstoke, its ancient walls surrounded by a picturesque moat (*inset*). Built in the 14th century by William de Clinton, Earl of Huntingdon, and later to become the ancestral home of the Dilke family (now the Fetherston-Dilkes), it has a massive turreted gatehouse and octagonal towers at each corner, in one of which Richard III is said to have stayed before the Battle of Bosworth Field in 1485.

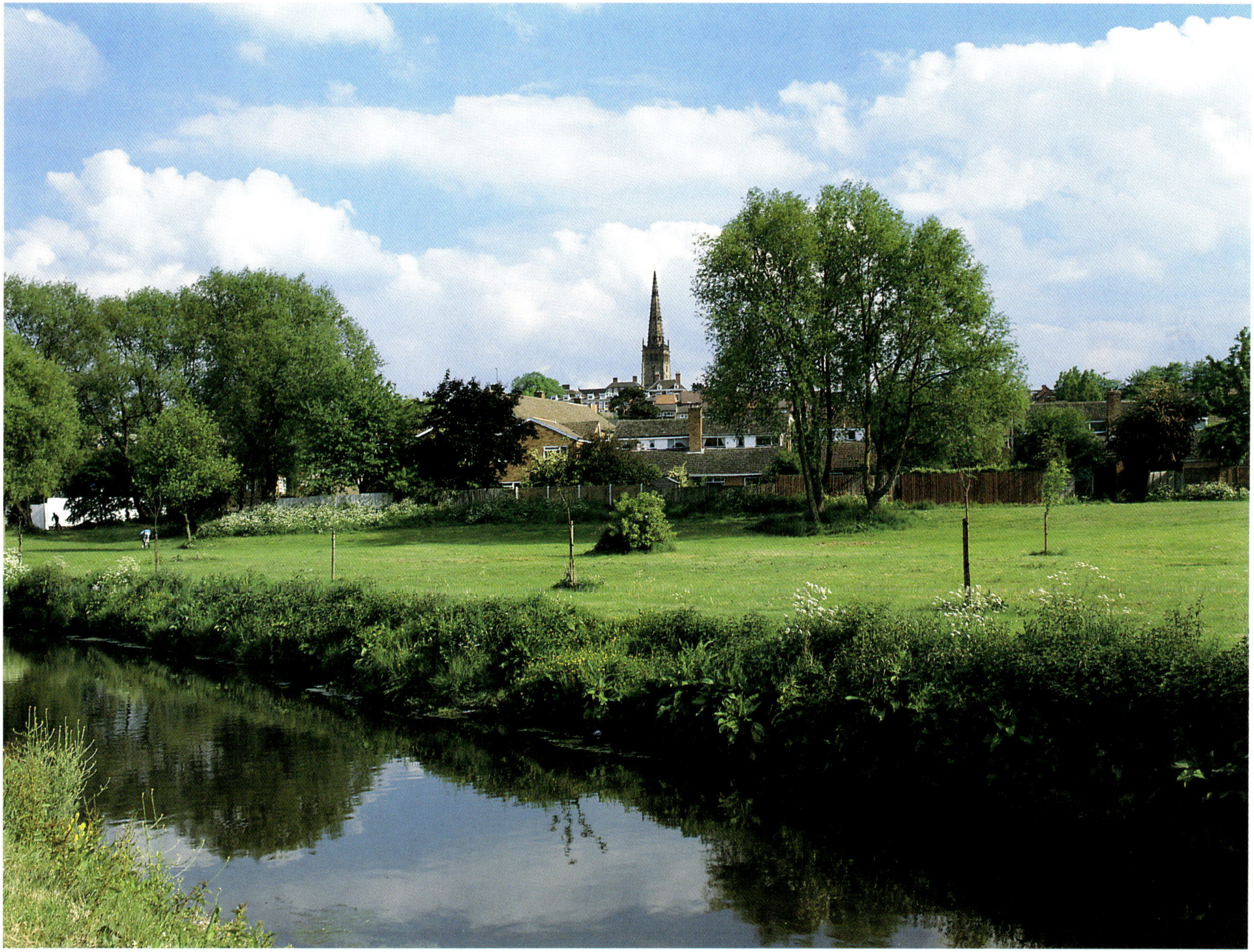

Nuneaton

There's no mistaking that Nuneaton is intensely proud of the fact that Mary Ann Evans was born in the town and lived there for 21 years. She's better known, of course, as the 19th-century novelist George Eliot, a male pseudonym she adopted at a time when female writers were taken less than seriously.

Nuneaton, now administratively linked to its near neighbour Bedworth, can trace its origins back to a Saxon settlement on the river Anker, and in more recent times it made a considerable name for itself in the weaving and coal-mining industries. But nowadays, having developed into one of Warwickshire's most go-ahead modern towns with a diverse commercial and industrial life, it is George Eliot who takes centre stage.

She borrowed and thinly disguised many locations in and around Nuneaton for her books, and these associations are proudly preserved. The parish church of St Nicolas is Milby church in *Scenes of Clerical Life*; the George Eliot Hotel (once the Bull) is the Red Lion in *Janet's Repentance*; nearby Astley church is Knebley church in *Mr Gilfil's Love Story*; Chilvers Coton church, where the writer was baptised, is Shepperton church in *Scenes of Clerical Life*; and historic Arbury Hall, ancestral home of the Newdegate family, is Cheverel Manor in *Mr Gilfil's Love Story*. The links are too numerous for all to be listed.

George Eliot was born at Arbury Farm (now South Farm) in 1819, shortly before the family moved to Griff House (now a restaurant), where she grew up. Many aspects of the house and its garden, as well as members of her family and the friends who influenced her childhood here, can be identified under different names in *Middlemarch*, *Adam Bede*, *The Mill on the Floss*, and other stories.

Nuneaton even has a hospital named after George Eliot, its wards identified by the names of her characters, and there's a George Eliot Memorial Garden too. At the heart of the shopping centre, a splendid bronze statue of her, by the sculptor John Letts, was unveiled in 1984 *(inset)*.

One of Nuneaton's principal attractions is Riversley Park, its colourful riverside gardens providing a fine setting for the town's Museum and Art Gallery *(opposite)*, opened in 1917 and imaginatively modernised in recent years. Not unexpectedly, one of its principal exhibition areas is devoted to the life and times of George Eliot.

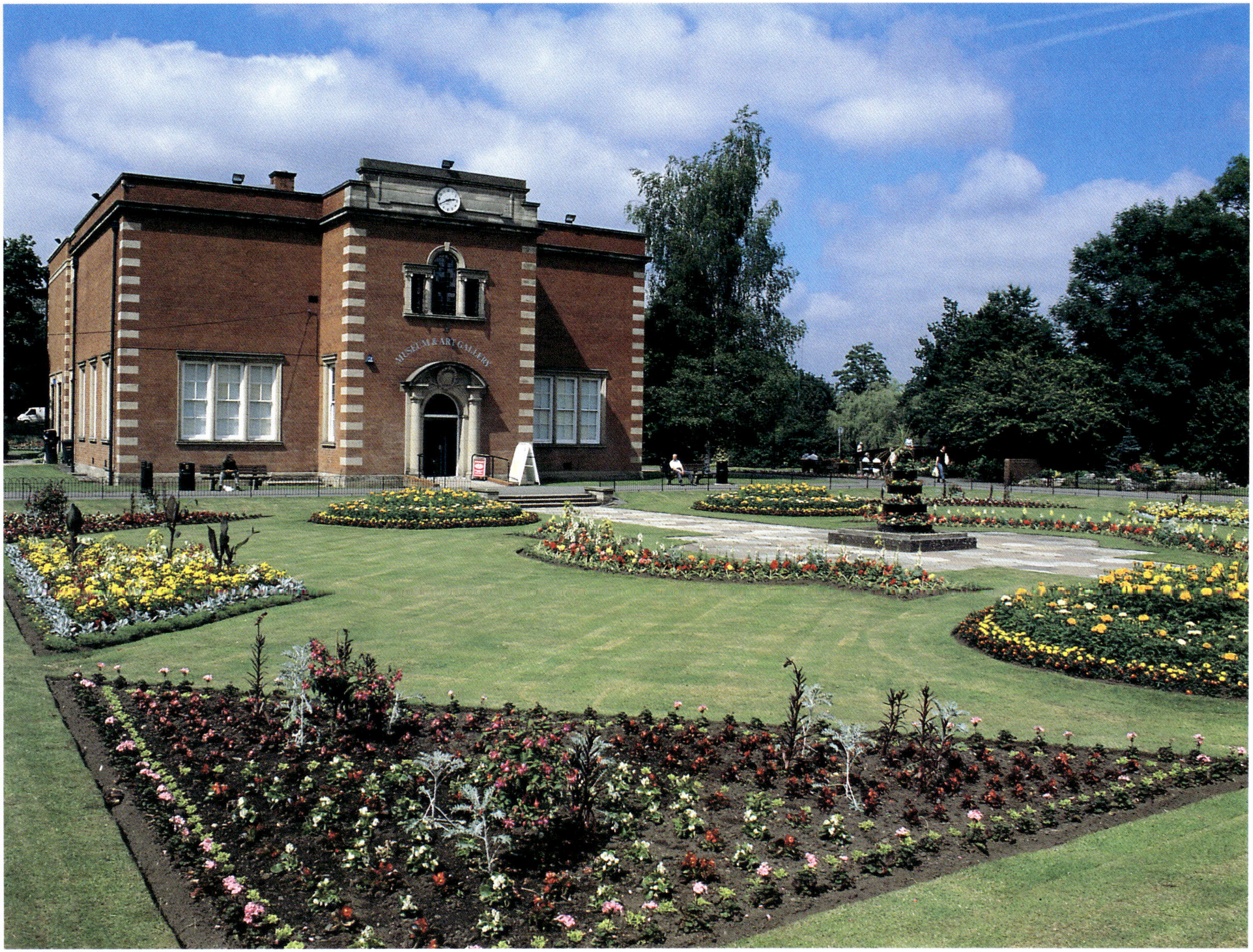
MUSEUM & ART GALLERY

Sutton Park

The City of Birmingham has many notable possessions, but there can surely be none to rival the inestimable value of Sutton Park (*opposite*). It was in 1974 that controversial boundary changes extended Birmingham's influence to include Sutton Coldfield and its famous park, and the acquisition gave the city one of the most remarkable municipal open spaces in the Midlands, if not in the entire country. It is remarkable because its 2,500 acres of unspoilt, open countryside, woodland and lakes survive virtually unscathed on the very edge of the vast Midlands conurbation, with Birmingham and its suburbs literally within walking distance.

The park's history can be traced back many centuries, and it was once part of an extensive royal forest and chase, the haunt of monarchs and noblemen. In 1527, John Vesey, Bishop of Exeter and a native of Sutton Coldfield, obtained from Henry VIII a charter which gave the park to the local inhabitants. It was one of those beneficent acts for which the bishop is still remembered in Sutton Coldfield today, another being the founding of the famous school which bears his name.

Nowadays, Sutton Park's visitors can be counted in their hundreds of thousands each year, and they come not only to enjoy the vast open spaces of moorland and heathland, the lakes (*inset*) and the great tracts of unspoilt forest, but to indulge in the many leisure and sporting activities which the park has to offer. Fortunately (at least as far as motorists are concerned), cars are allowed on many of the park's roads, a fact which provides a rare and unlikely opportunity for a leisurely drive in richly varied countryside actually within the bounds of the City of Birmingham. Wildlife enthusiasts are in their element here, and archaeological historians also have more than a passing interest, as the course of the great Roman highway known as Ryknild Street can be traced near the park's western boundary.

Sutton Park has hosted many notable events in its time, and has even provided one of the key stages in the RAC's gruelling international rally, but arguably the most memorable occasion was in 1957 when the International Scout Jamboree was held here. More than 35,000 scouts from all over the world converged on the park to be met by the Queen and Duke of Edinburgh, and a plaque on a stone plinth commemorates the event.

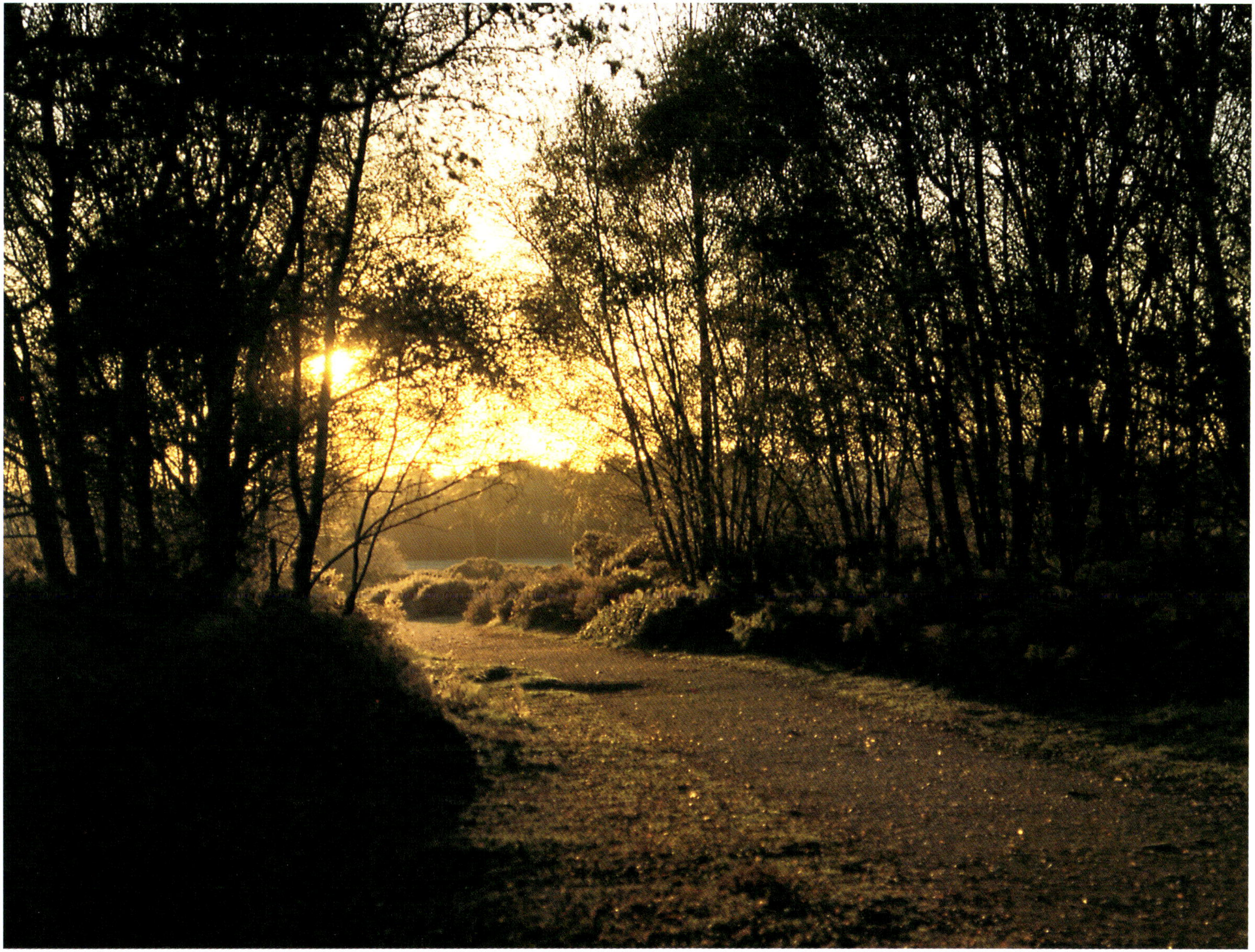

Polesworth and Atherstone

To outsiders at least, a popular conception about Warwickshire, particularly since it lost some of its largest centres of population to the County of West Midlands, is that its main interest is now chiefly confined to its southern half. It comes as something of a surprise to those who know little of the county, that the northern half embraces historic towns and villages no less interesting than their southern counterparts.

Nuneaton, featured earlier, is an obvious example, and so are Polesworth and Atherstone. Polesworth, in fact, is one of the county's most ancient communities, and it was already a flourishing settlement by the river Anker when King Egbert founded a Benedictine abbey here, and his daughter, Editha, became the first abbess. The parish church is dedicated to her, and is all that remains of the old abbey, although the gatehouse still survives as one of Polesworth's numerous architectural treasures. Another is the battlemented mansion of Pooley Hall, built by Sir Thomas Cockayne in 1509, which looks out over the town from its vantage point above the Coventry Canal.

It was mining subsidence which created the nearby nature reserve known as Alvecote Pools. Here, the quiet waters of the Anker, after flowing beneath Polesworth's fine multi-arched bridge (*opposite*), widen out after a couple of miles to fill the low-lying land, providing a haven for wildlife and a wealth of interest for nature lovers.

Not far to the south-east of Polesworth is Atherstone, historically a major centre of the hatting industry, which straddles the Roman Watling Street, better known today as the A5. This busy highway now bypasses the town, leaving the old Roman section as Atherstone's mile-long main thoroughfare, aptly called Long Street. This is the scene of the Atherstone Ball Game each Shrove Tuesday, a somewhat bizarre tradition dating back to medieval times.

Atherstone was also an important stopping-place for stagecoaches, and several of the town's existing hostelries were coaching inns. At the heart of the town is the old market square, where a twice-weekly market is still held, watched over by the historic parish church of St Mary (*inset*) with its distinctive Gothic-style tower.

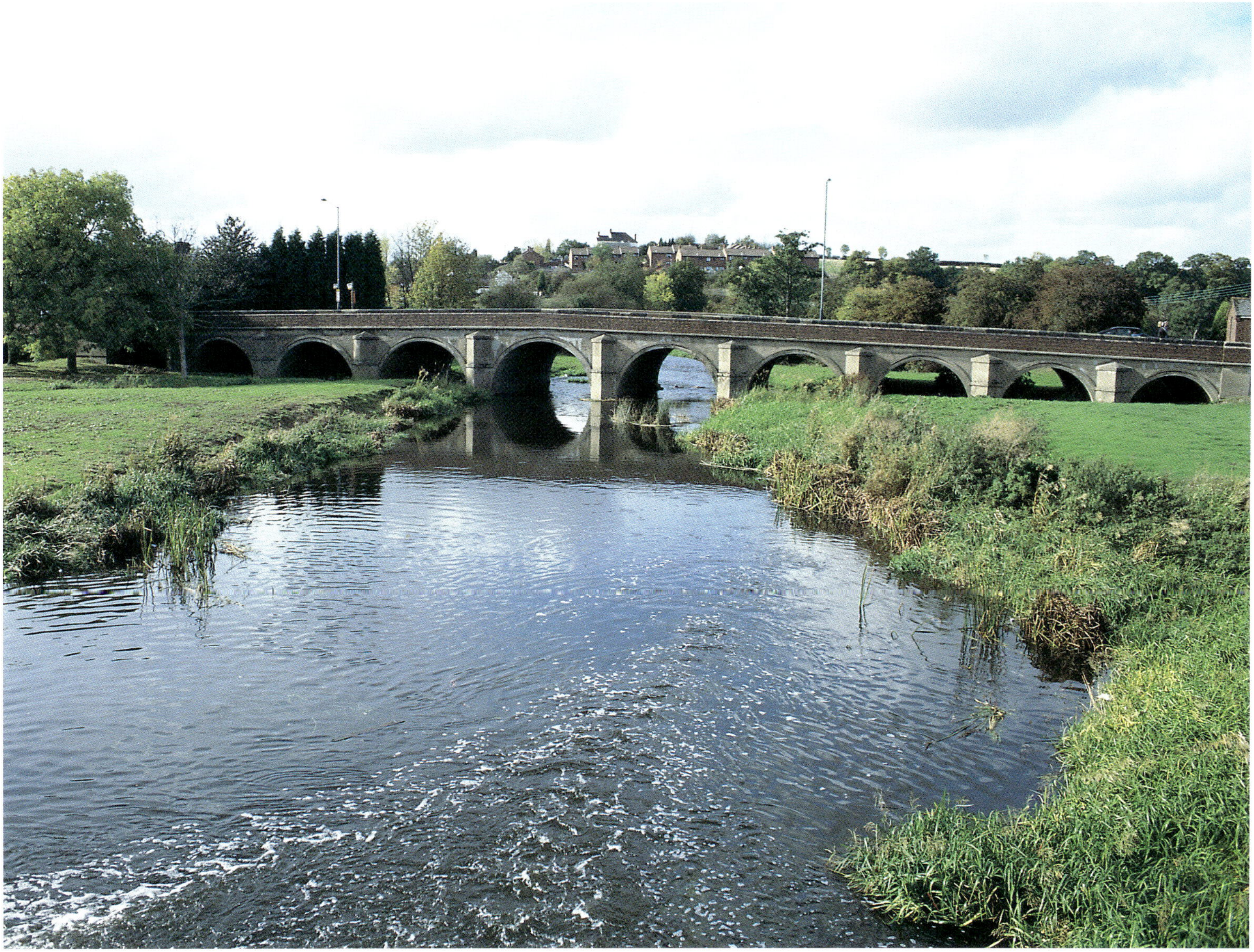

Newton Regis

When the motorway builders constructed the M42 north-eastwards from Birmingham, they could so easily have scarred Newton Regis irreparably. As it is, the motorway misses the village by a few hundred yards, leaving the villagers with nothing more sinister than the constant hum of distant traffic, as a reminder that it's there. Newton Regis *(opposite)* thus lives on as a place of considerable charm - the most northerly village in Warwickshire if one discounts the little hamlet of No Man's Heath by the county boundary a couple of miles away.

In an age when traditional English village life is under constant threat, Newton Regis can count itself fortunate. It still possesses its post office and shop, a thriving school, a popular 400-year-old village inn and a vibrant spirit of community. It has its visual attractions too, including picturesque old cottages, a sprinkling of thatch and half-timbering, and a willow-fringed village pond *(inset)*. The disconcertingly itinerant habits of the pond's resident ducks have necessitated the erection of two unusual 'beware of the ducks' road signs, as a warning to passing motorists.

At one end of the village rises the slender spire of the parish church of St Mary, in which Charles I is said to have prayed on his way to fight in the Civil War battle at the neighbouring village of Seckington. But it was not this particular kingly visit which gave Newton Regis the royal suffix to its name. The honour was bestowed by Henry II as long ago as 1159, when the area was part of a royal manor. King's Newton was an early variation, but the grander-sounding Newton Regis won the day. At one time, the village was also quaintly known as Newton-in-the-Thistles, a name which alluded to the abundance of locally grown thistles used for the carding of flax in the production of linen. The looms on which the linen was once woven were housed in what is now the village inn.

Today the inhabitants of Newton Regis no doubt find it strange to realise that their village once supported busy weavers, let alone its own tailors, shoemakers, wheelwrights, carpenters, butchers and a grocer. The effect of evolution on the rural way of life needs no further illustration.

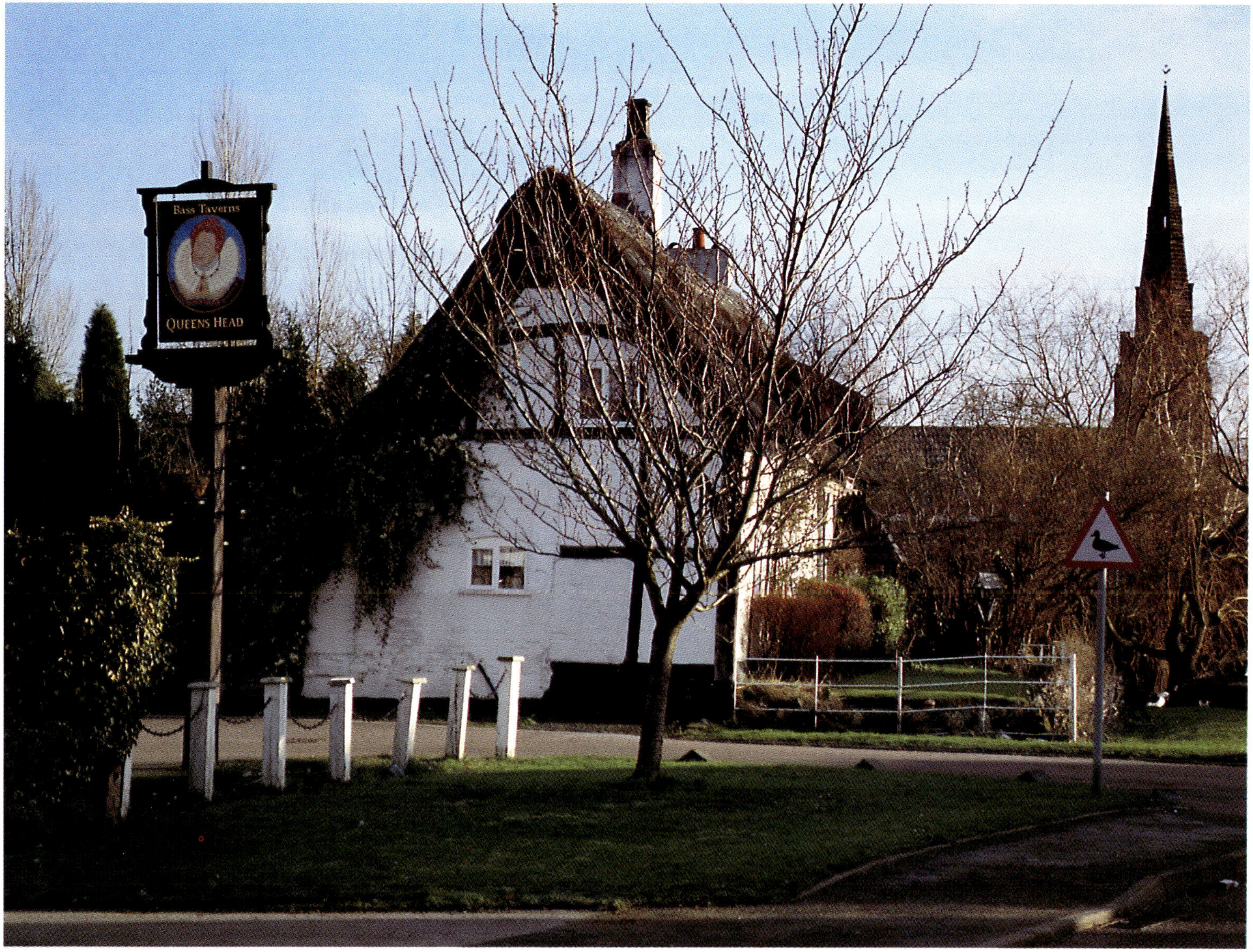
Bass Taverns
QUEENS HEAD